THE *JACKWAGON* BANDWAGON

"Tim Hawkins is not right in the head, and neither are you because you picked up this book. If you want to feel more normal, read this and laugh at him. I dared Tim to write this book, taunting him that he was only capable of writing 140 characters at time. Good job, Tim! Homeschooling works! (Please check my spelling. I went to public school.)"

—KERRI POMAROLLI, COMEDIAN, AUTHOR OF
Moms' Night Out and Other Things I Miss

"Thanks to Tim, I see that the 'Now I Lay Me Down to Sleep' kids prayer is more horrifying than anything Alice Cooper ever wrote. Tim is that guy who says everything you've ever thought but were never clever enough to come up with yourself. Ridiculously hilarious."

—SEAN COLELLI, ALICE COOPER'S SOLID ROCK
TEEN CENTER, PHOENIX, ARIZONA

"Tim's refreshingly honest and family-friendly take on the many humorous parts of life will have you laughing from start to finish. Our family couldn't put it down! You'll be reading *Diary of a Jackwagon* out loud for the whole family to enjoy."

—RICK SANTORUM, PRESIDENTIAL CANDIDATE, FORMER
US SENATOR, COAUTHOR OF *Bella's Gift*

"I first met Tim and saw him perform in 2008, and I've been a raving fan ever since. Tim's insights are dead-center accurate, and his stand-up comedy is cleverly hilarious. I know that like me you'll find this book entertaining, perceptive, and too much fun to only read once."

—C. NORWOOD DAVIS, CFO, THE JOHN MAXWELL COMPANY

"*Diary of a Jackwagon* is comedy caffeine in print. With an amazing goofball wit, Hawkins liberates our inner Jr. Higher, gives a loud raspberry to our personal Pharisee, and provides much needed exercise to those long dormant belly-laugh muscles. I plan to send a copy of this book to every humorless sourpuss and 'get off my lawn' acquaintance I know."

—RICK BUNDSCHUH, COAUTHOR OF *Soul Surfer*, KAUAI, HAWAII

"I've never seen a performer command a stage like Tim Hawkins. Tim goes from 0 to 60 lightning fast, and the audience stays with him from the opener through the finale. He is quite simply one of the most talented comedians in any genre out there today. From parody songs to stand-up bits to audience interaction, he's phenomenal. And I'm a fan."

—MICHAEL W. SMITH, RECORDING ARTIST

"*Diary of a Jackwagon* takes us deeper into the thoughts of a man who finds the funny in yoga pants, Snickaloafs, and Noah's Ark painted in our kids' bedrooms. I put Tim in the same league with Dave Barry and Erma Bombeck as an American humorist. In a world full of overused superlatives: Not reading this book? THAT is the worst!"

—MIKE ALLEY, 95.1 SHINE-FM AND 48LIVE PRODUCTIONS

"When we first booked Tim for a concert at our church, a client testimonial on his website warned that attendees might 'pee their pants' due to laughter. A vulgar endorsement, right? As a physician, I was pleased that there was indeed an increased demand for incontinence medications after the show. After reading *Diary of a Jackwagon*, Tim's comedy will once again be very good for my business."

—BRANDON WEBB M.D., FAMILY PHYSICIAN, LINCOLN, NEBRASKA

"Tim may be low on blinker fluid, but his songs and jokes make our family laugh till we cry. All hail Mr. Yoga Pants!"

—KIRK CAMERON, ACTOR, PRODUCER

"If you think that great comedy always comes from a tortured soul, Tim Hawkins will prove you wrong. I laughed till I passed out reading this book. I have had the pleasure of personally meeting some of the comedic greats including Steve Martin, Bill Hicks, and Sam Kinison. Tim is without reservation one of the finest comedians of our generation."

—JOHN BLEDSOE, SPEAKER, ESTATE PLANNER,
AUTHOR OF *The Gospel of Roth*

"I'm proud to join in the Brotherhood of Jackwagons everywhere! In concert and in this book, I laugh so hard at Tim and think 'As a husband, dad, and everyday guy, Tim sure is some kind of jackwagon.' About two heartbeats later it occurs to me. . . . 'Oh no! He's talking about ME!'"

—TIM HATTRICK, *The Tim and Willy Radio Show*, PHOENIX, ARIZONA

"Tim has a refreshing take on everyday moments that make you approach life with a more playful lens. If you need a good laugh, this is the book to pick up and read."

—MILES McPHERSON, SENIOR PASTOR, ROCK
CHURCH, SAN DIEGO, CALIFORNIA

"What if we could get inside the mind of Tim Hawkins? At home with family and on the tour bus, Hawkins is constantly capturing the stuff that makes people laugh. "

—TIM DeTELLIS, PRESIDENT, NEW MISSIONS, ORLANDO, FLORIDA

"Tim and I must be related, I thought. Then I saw him perform in concert for nearly 5,000 people and realized something: Tim makes everyone feel that way. I'm grateful that he has finally written a book so that I can get a Tim fix whenever I need it."

—GARY DIXON, EXECUTIVE DIRECTOR, NORTHWEST
MINISTRY CONFERENCE, SEATTLE, WASHINGTON

"Tim connects with his audience like most public people never do. I wondered how Tim's stand-up style would translate to the written word. Answer? It's absolutely delightful and hysterical. You can enjoy this book bit by bit or all in one sitting. And please, don't test out any of the lyrics from 'Things You Don't Say to Your Wife.' Take my word for it."

—KEN DAVIS, COMEDIAN, AUTHOR OF *Fully Alive*

"Tim has an uncanny way of putting his slightly skewed twist on our everyday routines to create comedy genius that connects with us all. Generally, I shy away from any book that I can't color, but I made an exception for *Jackwagon*. I may never pick up a crayon again."

—DAN RUPPLE, PRODUCER, WRITER, FOUNDING MEMBER
OF ISAAC AIR FREIGHT COMEDY TROUPE

"Tim is on the short list of men my children like more than me. He absolutely has given our whole family countless hours of entertainment with his stand-up comedy and songs like 'Chick-fil-A.' Plus, we can't figure out if he looks more like Dale Earnhardt Jr. or the guy from *Sister Wives*."

—BOB STURM, *The Bob and Dan Radio Show*,
SPORTSRADIO 1310 THE TICKET, DALLAS, TEXAS

"While reading these pages I felt guilty laughing, like when the kid falls on his face in the school play. It's sad but it's true and it's funny . . . so I laughed. I keep wondering if Tim will snap out of it one day. This book is comedy gold!"

—PETE BRISCOE, SENIOR PASTOR, BENT TREE
BIBLE FELLOWSHIP, CARROLLTON, TEXAS

"When you read *Diary of a Jackwagon*, you expect Tim to be nuts. And then you realize he is. The way he links thoughts together is brilliant. Tim actually puts into words what many others (some of whom are confined to an institution) are unwilling or unable to say. You absolutely must read this book and catch a glimpse of how Tim thinks. It's a bit scary!"

—BILL GRAENING, DIRECTOR, ALIVE FESTIVAL

"*Funny, hilarious, ridiculous* are the first three words that come to mind. I have never laughed so long or so many times. Read and get ready."

"There is a guitar-string thin line between lunatic jester and genius saint. *Jackwagon* is a joy to read as Tim dances on that line. What C. S. Lewis did for the formation of critical thinking in the faith, Tim Hawkins does to allow us to see the hilarious side of God in reality. If you've always wanted to believe God actually created laughter, this book is a MUST read."

"There are some people you just connect with instantly. Tim Hawkins is one of those people. I found myself laughing out loud reading *Diary of a Jackwagon*."

"We are made in the image of God, but deep down we all know that the gene pool was contaminated by the time we were born. That's why the best comedy makes us laugh at ourselves. There is probably not a weirder group of people than Christians. I should know. I lead them. The beautiful thing about Christians laughing at ourselves is that it helps us lighten up and not act better than the rest of the world. I can only imagine Jesus reading this book. He is laughing so hard. I imagine a snort."

"Tim is the most outrageous, outlandish guy we've seen at our annual #LFLGala. Edmonton loves Tim!"

Diary OF A JACKWAGON

TIM HAWKINS
WITH JOHN DRIVER

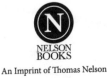

NELSON BOOKS

An Imprint of Thomas Nelson

Published in Nashville, Tennessee, by Nelson Books, an imprint of Thomas Nelson. Nelson Books and Thomas Nelson are registered trademarks of HarperCollins Christian Publishing, Inc.

Published in association with the literary agency of Wolgemuth & Associates, Inc.

Thomas Nelson titles may be purchased in bulk for educational, business, fund-raising, or sales promotional use. For information, please e-mail SpecialMarkets@ThomasNelson.com.

Unless otherwise noted, Scripture quotations are taken from the New Revised Standard Version of the Bible. © 1989 by the Division of Christian Education of the National Council of the Churches of Christ in the U.S.A. All rights reserved.

Library of Congress Cataloging-in-Publication Data

Hawkins, Tim, 1968-
  Diary of a Jackwagon / Tim Hawkins.
    pages cm
  ISBN 978-0-7180-0629-7
1. Hawkins, Tim, 1968- 2. Comedians--United States--Biography. I. Title.
  PN2287.H3335A3 2014
  792.702'8092--dc23
  [B]

2014041748

Printed in the United States of America

15 16 17 18 19 RRD 6 5 4 3 2 1

CONTENTS

Contents

FOREWORD

BY BUBBA WATSON

A couple of years ago, a friend asked me if I had heard of the comedian Tim Hawkins. I said no and he pulled out his phone and immediately started searching for Tim Hawkins's "Chick-fil-A song," insisting that I had to see it right away. He was right; I did need to see it. The first time I heard the song I couldn't believe how funny, and true, it was. It was like Tim knew about my secret craving for Chick-fil-A every Sunday. I was instantly hooked on Tim's comedy and started telling everyone I knew about him. I even started slipping into the PING equipment trailer at tournaments just to watch Tim's videos on their computer.

Before long, I had watched most of his songs and stand-up bits, listening to classics such as "The Government Can" and "Inappropriate Wedding Songs" over and over and over again. I still laugh every time I hear them. When I am playing on the PGA Tour, referencing Tim's songs has even become an inside joke between my caddie and me. For example, if we have an early tee time, one of us is almost always going to say "who can tax the sunrise, the government can!" When I hit a drive into the woods (which happens a little too often) it is also fun to mimic Tim's son and say, "I will feed you to the fire ants!"

While I loved Tim's work from the start, as I learned more about him I really began to appreciate just how different he is from many of the other well-known comedians. When you watch his shows or listen to his songs you don't need to look around and see who is listening. Having a young family, I am very aware that what we watch on TV or listen to on the radio reflects on us personally. Kids are like glue and bad language sticks to them too. It's good to know that Tim's comedy is acceptable for everyone. He also proves that bad language and adult content are not requirements to be funny.

Another reason that Tim's work is special to me is that after watching, listening, and learning about Tim's life, I found out that he is a Christian. When I was younger the idea of a comedian being a Christian seemed strange. I thought Christians were supposed to be simple, straightforward, and boring. But as I have grown as a Christian myself, I have realized that my old perceptions were not true. Tim is proof that people can have fun, be entertaining, and be Christians all at the same time.

The truth is, I am not a "Christian golfer." I am a Christian, and I am a golfer. One is who I am. The other is what I do. To me, Tim Hawkins is not a "Christian comedian." One is definitely who he is, and the other is definitely something he does very well—an opinion anyone who reads this book will share regardless of how they feel about faith. Trust me, this guy is funny.

So funny it'll make ya wanna slap ya mama.

INTRODUCTION

A book by me? A bound block of paper pages (or a giga-byte of digital pages that they make to look like pages, but are not actually pages at all) with little words by Tim Hawkins printed on them? What exactly are these babblings you have stumbled upon? The inner monologue of a madman? The metaphorical midnight tip-ping of a comedy cow? The random musings of a comedic observer?

The answer to at least one of these is—well, yes. You bet your sweet bippy. I'm not a betting man. And I don't own a bippy. Never have. Don't even know what that means. It would be a weird conver-sation to overhear in Vegas, though.

"Hey, who's that guy at the roulette wheel?"

"I'm not sure. But he just bet his bippy."

"What? Are you serious?"

"I am."

"Sweet."

"That's right. That man just bet his sweet bippy."

But yes. The answer is yes. I'm not sure I actually remember the question. So back to the babblings, I guess. You are about to read a book of excerpts from my extremely private comedy journal. Here's the deal: for the past twenty years, I have been writing almost everything down that I think is funny. That doesn't necessarily mean others think it is funny, but then again, I don't necessarily care about the simple basic rules of social etiquette or that annoyingly over-enforced rule that says I have to drive on the right side of the road and stay seated while I do so.

People often ask me how I write comedy. It's simple. I didn't say easy. I said simple. I listen a lot, and I write everything down. Then I come back to it later to see if I can find the funny. Sometimes it works. Sometimes, meh . . . not so much.

Point being, when I come across something funny, my personal process is to find anything I can to write on and capture the moment. Kmart receipts. Napkins. Toilet paper. Gum wrappers. Tiny strips of paper that come out of corporate document shredders. Bread sticks. Garden hoses. A waiter's white dress shirt—while he is still wearing it. They really should come up with better ways to take notes.

But for now, you are about to read random pieces of my comedy journal over the past twenty years. And when I say random, I mean I didn't even take the time to arrange the entries in chronological order. You're welcome. Some things you may recognize from my shows and some you may not. You may have never even seen one of my shows— or in other words, you may be a normal law-abiding citizen. I intend to change that right here. Right now. (Cue motivational mental Van Halen soundtrack—or the Pepsi One commercial from the 1990s.)

I've been told the top three best-selling books of all time (besides the Bible) are: 1) *The Purpose Driven Life*, 2) *Left Behind*, and 3) *Everyone Poops*. I'm not sure this book will come in fourth place, but you never know until you try, which ironically enough would've been a perfect subtitle for *Everyone Poops*.

You see, I do comedy for a living. You heard me right: a living. Trust me, most days I am as amazed as you are—especially since I'm just a jackwagon. Sometimes people treat me like I'm some kind of rock star, but I think that's silly. I'm no rock star. I just like to laugh with people, knowing we're all the same. We're no different. The only difference between me and you is that I have a microphone. And talent. Those are the only two things that separate me from you com-moners. So yes, I do this for a living, and it's some of those "living" parts I'm about to babble on about. Family. Culture. Music. Parenting. Education. And yes, perhaps even the occasional bippy.

Don't we all have people in our lives that we're not quite sure why they're in our lives? People you just have to stop and ask, "Why do I know you? Just get out. Get out . . . Mom." Yep, too many people in my life already, which is why I also have no desire to be famous—I have enough trouble dealing with people I know. Like know-it-alls. Those people who read something on the Internet and then patiently wait for social get-togethers, as these provide prime opportunities to release their worthless knowledge on innocent partygoers.

"Avocado? It's a fruit. Yep, a fruit. Tomato. It's a fruit." Look, if it can't be a Starburst flavor, it ain't a fruit. Okay, smacky? That's my little fruit test.

Or these people who use superlatives for everything. That's the "best." That's "absolutely amazing." "This deer sausage is unbelievable." Really? Unbelievable? Now if a bald eagle wearing a tuxedo swooped down and dropped a piece of deer sausage in your mouth? Yeah, that would be unbelievable. Because that's a bald eagle wearing a tux dropping deer sausage into your gob. You don't see that every day. Unless you're a homeschooler. They see things like that all the time. I'm talking about a normal person. Here's all I'm saying: that piece of meat, while delicious, is extremely believable.

Or the phrase "That's the worst." If you live in the first world, I don't think you should be allowed to say "That's the worst" about anything in your life. My wife and I dropped our daughter off at the mall recently and her friends weren't there yet to meet her. So my daughter was like, "Oh no, my friends aren't here yet and I can't go shopping because they might show up and I won't be here to meet them." And my wife said to her, "I know, honey, that's the worst."

I grabbed my Kmart receipt and a pen. This was going to be good.

That's the worst? Being stuck in the mountains in twenty feet of snow or being lost at sea with a bloody leg while dozens of hungry sharks slowly encircle your soon-to-be carcass? That doesn't place you in a little more of a pickle? Nope. Not the worst.

Remember those Chilean miners? Those dudes that got stuck

down in that mine for like thirty days? I can hear one of them now in a very thick Chilean drawl . . .

"Oh no. This? This is not good. This is not good at all. We been down here a long time. I've lost track of the days. But we got no food. We got no water. We don't got a lot of air left. We may not live to see another day. This? This is the worst."

He painfully pauses for a moment, but is brought back by another thought. "The only thing that I can think of that is worse than this? You know sometimes . . . when you're at the mall? And your friends are not there to meet you yet? And you can't go shopping 'cause they might show up and not know where you are? So you got to wait on the curb for like ten minutes? Wow. You know, I shouldn't be complaining right now. I should count my blessings, you know? Because—don't get me wrong—this is bad. This is really bad. But that? Waiting at the mall for your friends? That is the worst!"

Famous? No, slow down, cowboy. Unbelievable? Perhaps. Still, you won't find any of these superfluous superlatives tagging along behind these babblings.

The worst? Nah. And I do have some good news for you. More likely than not, this book will not be the worst thing you've ever read.

Unless, of course, you had to pay full retail for it. That may be the worst. But sorry, my kids need to go to college and not ring up so much debt that their children will be putting cardboard inside their shoes. So thanks. You're the best. Well, sort of.

BLINKER FLUID

They say the best things in life are free. Well, whoever "they" are, they have obviously never tried to walk out of a Walmart with one of those cool *Duck Dynasty* shirts—with Uncle Si's huge beard plastered from top to bottom like a follicular monument to rednecks everywhere—without paying for it. Don't say the customer is always right if you don't mean it.

I never knew Walmart security guards were trusted by their superiors to wield such potent Tasers. Perhaps I missed my calling, because from my vantage point of that greasy tile floor while convulsing in an electrically charged puddle of my own urine, those security guys looked like they were having a lot of fun.

Negative. The best things in life are not free. In fact, they cost you plenty. Just ask my wife. Marrying me may have started off as a pretty inexpensive endeavor, but years in a marriage are like compounded interest. The cost, and some might even say the rewards, accrue at a different level than "normal" non-married life. My wife has been accruing from our marriage for over twenty years. For her, the cost has been high. Dollars. Years. Sanity.

For me? I'm like an A-list frequent flyer with endless rewards and benefits. This marriage thing is the jackpot. I get free drinks and she even helps me fasten my seat belt. "Emergency exits are located here and here and . . . oh, just keep listening to your headphones, you deadbeat! I'll do all the work anyway."

Yep, I got the better end of this deal and it only sweetens with each passing year. I hope she never figures it out. Seriously, she doesn't need me at all. If she ever leaves me, I'm going with her. If you're a husband, then you know what I'm talking about. Most of the time, we just walk around the house wondering to ourselves, *Why are we here?* I feel like a catcher in T-ball.

I know this to be true, but I still find a way to be offended at the way my wife speaks to me: like I'm some sort of child. Look, I get it. I am a child. But you don't have to be so rude about it. I do stuff around here, too, you know. Well, not really. But that's not the point.

I don't think I'm the only man out there facing this criss-crossed communication dilemma between truth and embarrassment. Sometimes I will be out with my wife at a restaurant or party and I will witness the same communication between other well-meaning females and their victimized masculine counterparts. It is an epidemic and it is high time someone stands up and sounds the alarm for the hairy ones everywhere. We are just men. If you prick us, do we not bleed?

On a side note, please keep the pricking to the confines of the metaphorical, because as you have proven on countless occasions with your incessant picking at our every random zit and blemish, we do bleed pretty easily. The question was rhetorical, you sadistic animals.

The point is that women talk to men like we're idiots. We are not idiots. The greatest evidence of this kind of humiliating communication comes from the female propensity to use excessive hand gestures in addition to words. I see it all the time in my house. Just the other day, my wife, Heather, said, "Honey, go get me a box."

Now to any normal adult English-speaking human on the planet, these words would have sufficed. I may not be the sharpest knife in the drawer, but I do have a pretty proficient working knowledge of basic shapes. Circles. Squares. Triangles. Yep, I'm a real Pythagoras—you know, his theorem and whatnot.

But apparently my wife did not agree with the fact that I have mastered my shapes. Thus her words, "Go get me a box," were accompanied by a fully dramatized hand pantomime of what a box looks like—the quick movements of her knuckles and fingers striking sharp, imaginary right angles in the air, outlining the delicate borders of the mystery shape. And I don't mean just once or twice. She persisted for some twenty seconds to make imaginary square shapes out of the various repositioning of her hands. She was like Madonna striking a pose—minus the pointy bra and ridiculous fake British accent, of course. I'm the only one who uses those in our home.

It was a foolproof visual aid—and also proof that to her I must be a fool. Why else would she need to resort to shadow puppetry to assist the slower, hairier hearer? She continued to whisper the word "box," each syllable of her slowly worded, obviously-meant-for-an-idiot sentence continuing to rest upon the visual aid of her happy hands.

I turned my head to one side and opened my mouth real wide. "Uuummm, do you mean a boooox? Me no know shapes good." I then let out the loudest donkey bray I could muster while dancing around the living room making horns on my head with my fingers. How's that for hand gestures?

Unimaginably, she had the audacity to be offended at my reaction. In fact, she returned another hand gesture I was not anticipating. You see? This kind of stuff has to stop. Men are real people too. In fact, there are a lot of things I would like to see women do without us. I know they like the idea of doing things without us because I see it on their bumper stickers all the time. So help me if I see one more white Jetta with a bumper sticker that reads, "Who needs men when we have chocolate?"

Next time you have a hole in the drywall, go get a Kit Kat bar to fix that bad boy. See how that works out for you. Try snuggling up to a Baby Ruth on a cold night—sure the smell would be better, but overall, I think you'd miss the man. We have purpose, even if it is not that evident on a daily basis in our own homes. Men should not be discarded simply because the women do the lioness's share of the household duties.

Yes, we do the occasional spackling and painting. Yes, we kill the insects you so instinctively fear. Yes, we change the oil in the cars. Hey, this one is worth all the trouble we bring. The other day I sent my wife to get the oil changed at our local Jiffy Lube. She just couldn't take the pressure of the whole affair. I suppose it's the bombardment of greasy clipboards and questions. Air filters. Wiper blades. Vacuumed floor-boards. You know, everything but the actual oil itself. She turned a thirty-dollar oil change into a six-hundred-dollar overhaul.

I got the bill and responded as any concerned Neanderthal would. "Uh, honey? What is this?"

She shot back at me a squinted look of absolute disgust. "Well, funny you would ask now. If Jerry down at 'the Jif' had not been so concerned, I probably wouldn't be here right now."

"The Jif?"

"Yes, Tim! Those of us who pay attention . . ." She spoke slowly while gently knocking on my forehead as if a magic door might open to another dimension. I love it when she does that. She continued, ". . . we know that 'the Jif' saves lives!"

"It does, does it?"

"Don't start with me, Tim. Jerry said we were totally out of blinker fluid. Oh my gosh! And I've been driving around this city for how long? Did you ever think to check the blinker fluid? Do you want me to die? Is that your plan?"

Yeah, some master plan that would be! Like she ever uses her turn signal anyway. Truth is, Jerry's master plan works a lot better: to bankrupt the Hawkins household over blinker fluid and lug nut butter. He and the Walmart guy must be in cahoots.

So chin up, Timmy boy. You know your wife is smarter than you. No doubts here. You know she works harder than you do. You know that she thinks you're an idiot. And yes, you know that she is right. But you, my friend, you do serve a purpose. Even if she does not always see it. Even if she doesn't vocalize it. You are still winning by a landslide.

And besides, no other area of need is greater than the actual time spent on the road itself. Without me around, I'm not sure what would happen out there on the highway. The other day, I allowed a rarity to happen: I let her drive and I rode shotgun in the passenger's seat. She had been driving for a while when she suddenly got the most curious look on her face.

"What's wrong?" I asked.

"These roads are horrible!"

I hardly had the heart to tell her that she had been driving on the rumble strip for fifteen minutes, yet I soon found the heart to do so. Yes, that is my role. Honesty. Especially when it is painful.

She honestly did not know what they were, bless her heart. So I gently explained that when you drive off the highway the rumble strip makes noise and vibrates to let you know to come back on the road. Her answer was both true and priceless—and proof that husbands everywhere do indeed serve a purpose, even from their position of household and intellectual inferiority. Like a Christmas tree, she lit up with excitement. "That is so awesome for blind people." You should take a break from this book now, find a nice shady tree, assume the lotus position, and meditate on that last line until you lose the feeling in your butt cheeks.

So rest well, oh husband within. Your role in the home—and especially in the car—is both safe and secure. And yes, sometimes the best things in life are indeed free. And they flow from the mouth of my lovely wife.

However, there are certain things we husbands should never say back to our wives. That's why I wrote this song to remind myself—to the tune of Green Day's "Good Riddance (Time of Your Life)." Sing along in your head as you read and try not to cry.

Things You Don't Say to Your Wife

Hey honey, have you gained some weight in your rear end?
That dress you wear reminds me of my old girlfriend
And where'd you get those shoes? I think they're pretty lame
Would you stop talking 'cause I'm trying to watch the game

If you're a man who wants to live a long and happy life
These are the things you don't say to your wife

I planned a hunting trip next week on your birthday
I didn't ask you 'cause I knew it'd be OK
Go make some dinner while I watch this fishing show
I taped it over our old wedding video

If you're a man who wants to live a long and happy life
These are the things you don't say to your wife

Your cooking is OK but not like mother makes
The diamond in the ring I bought you is a fake
Your eyes look puffy dear, are you feeling ill?
Happy anniversary! I bought you a treadmill

If you're a man who wants to live a long and happy life
These are the things you don't say to your wife
If you're a man who doesn't want to get killed with a knife
These are the things you don't say to your wife

I should probably add a small note of interest here. Throughout these ramblings, I will include some short thoughts for future tweets. I thought long and hard about a creative way to brand them and I came up with "Tweet Thought" . . . hey, I was having a rough week. At any rate, these are short, sweet tweets, so to tweet . . . or speak. Eh, you'll probably get the gist.

Tweet Thought @timhawkinscomic
Life is chess. The big dude can only move one square at a time and the queen gets to go wherever she wants.

Tweet Thought @timhawkinscomic
My wife taught me the difference between "Please don't go" and "Please. Don't. Go."

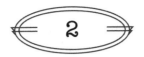

PLAYGROUNDS

Kids are the best. They deepen the meaning of life, reminding me of what's important and what is trivial. They keep me on my toes—and occasionally, they crush my toes with their Razor scooters. Nothing makes you feel more alive than a detached toenail. Yep, like I said, kids are the best.

Today I spent several hours at our local playground with my little ones. These playgrounds today are pretty spectacular. I'm not sure how they afford to hire NASA scientists to design them—perhaps I'm in the wrong business. I mean, these playlands are unbelievable feats of engineering. They are *huge*. Once I lost one of my kids on Play Platform Level Delta for a full two hours. Thankfully, I eventually found him in the room of balls just outside of the glass-blowing exhibit—it was near the emergency phones posted every hundred yards or so. He had pushed the button and their security center called my phone.

These modern playgrounds are monuments to the merits of molded plastic. Complete with drawbridges, towers, moats, boats, computer rooms, flight simulators, intercom systems, and drawing rooms (for stealing away during teatime, not for actual drawing . . . that's called the Drawing Quadrant down on level nine).

Oh yeah, monkey bars. Well, I don't think they call them that anymore. The National Association of Primate Businessmen got offended and threatened to pull their funding for future playground construction projects. I tell you what, those guys don't play around when it comes to their monkey business.

7

Some might even say that monkey business is no game. This makes me think of that fun fact my statistics professor always used to tell us: if you give a roomful of monkeys using typewriters an infinite amount of time, they could bang out the works of Shakespeare. I don't buy it. I'm convinced they couldn't come up with one sentence, what with the distracting screeching and poop throwing, although these haven't stopped me from writing this book.

When I was a kid, playgrounds were just a bit more primitive. They were built on cement or gravel or tiny pieces of broken glass, not on these soft Vitriturf floorings. This stuff today is like shredded rubber laced with shredded pillows laced with shredded lace. Hitting your head on the playground is like getting a relaxing temple massage. I should probably clarify that I am referring to the temples on the side of one's head, not the temples where people go to worship. That's another kind of temple massage that I know absolutely nothing about.

To my point, though, my kids love nothing more than to nosedive off the highest slide platform into the waterless pool of the playground floor. "Ooh Daddy, can I fall and smash my head again? It feels so dreamy." Sure, son, knock yourself out. If you can.

But in my day, we had no trouble knocking ourselves out. It was concrete. I sustained seven concussions just running to the water fountain—a water fountain that gave you tetanus, I might add. We also had some rides you no longer see on modern playgrounds, like the merry-go-round. There's a reason for that. There was nothing merry about the merry-go-round. It was more like the terror-go-round. The steel wheel of death. Yep, we had all kinds of names for it. You knew that ride was over when you were flung into the gravel. It was top choice for bullies who would always push you to get on it. "Come on, dude, you're going to love it!"

"I'm going to puke!" His point exactly. Mission accomplished. Score one for bullies everywhere.

I also have fond memories of the teeter-totter, or as some call it, the seesaw. That one taught us the concept of trust. It was like a double-sided human catapult. I remember it vividly. You sat down on—or rather, straddled—a hard wooden plank, thus positioning your most delicate parts for the highest potential of blunt force trauma. That's where the trust came in. As the other person entered the same vulnerable position by mounting the other end of the teeter-totter, the game was afoot—or as we veterans used to say on the playground, the game was acrotch.

If the two participants were both people of a reasonable disposition, it was the most fun imaginable. They could both be trusted to let the other push off with their legs and send their counterpart flying delightfully high in the air, and then the favor was returned vice versa. Maybe that's what they should have called the ride: the vice versa, emphasis on the vice.

But more oft than not, a kid of a reprobate mind would deceive his way onto one end of the teeter-totter and wait for his moment to attack. As I would joyously reach the pinnacle of the teeter, the villain would suddenly step off the totter, sending me careening crotchward toward the ground with the thrust of a blazing Patriot missile. From trust to thrust, it was now game over.

"Nice shot, dude," says Tim with the high-pitched Mickey Mouse voice. "I'll catch you guys later. Just going to head down to the emergency room for a bit. And while I'm down there, maybe I can get checked for hepatitis from the used cement sewer tubes I've been crawling around for all of my formative years."

Ah, but there was even greater carnage to be had on the medieval gauntlet that was my childhood playground. I remember the slide. Yep, that's the worst. Today's slides are usually made out of softer, more malleable materials like plastic. Ours? They were brutally forged into their shapes at hellishly high temperatures down at the steel mill. I envision a burly blacksmith beating the molten orange metal into submission for hours on end. Finally, he would remove his dark mask and wipe the gritty perspiration from his brow. A slide. Yep, our slides were made out of metal. What could go wrong?

Well, first of all, my most lasting memories of the slide come from those days when the temperatures reached into the hundreds. There it lay baking in the hot sun, just waiting for playful children to climb on and have some fun.

Now, when the temperatures are this high, children are not wearing their Sunday best or a pair of knickers. Nope, shorts are the only option for play. And in those days, we didn't have any of these Nike or Adidas athletic shorts made out of some high-tech polymer fabric that ensures safety and performance during playtime. No, we wore cut-off jean shorts—the ones with the white pockets sticking out of the bottom, which lets you know how short they were. It was a fashion statement we were more than willing to make.

After climbing the eight-foot ladder to the top, that ruddy young Tim Hawkins screamed to his brother below, "I'm ready!" To which his older evil brother, Todd, aware of what was about to happen, gave him an enthusiastic thumbs-up that all was clear and ready for sliding. He was the Cain to my Abel. The Esau to my Jacob.

I vaguely remember the entire experience—probably some sort of internal defense mechanism to guard my mental health. I do recall that about halfway down, I yelled out to Todd, "I smell something burning. What is that?" The rest of the memory consists of screaming amid a cloud of smoke as sparks flew out of my crotch. This must have been where they came up with the term "hot pants." Now I know the reason so many old guys walk so funny—they burned their butts off years ago on metal slides. It was the scourge of our generation.

But now that I think of it, that actually wasn't the worst part of it all. The worst was going home and having Mom spray Bactine all over my singed flesh. It was like aerosol salt in my wounds. Bactine was like the catchall medicine for every injury.

I can remember scraping up my knee—a minor scratch I could happily live with. "Roll up your pant leg. I'm going to spray some Bactine on it. I don't want you getting *gangrene!*"

"Aaahhh! It's burning my flesh off!"

10

"That just means it's working. It's penetrating and killing all that gunk."

"Killing the gunk? It's disintegrating my kneecap!"

"Oh, stop your screaming. You should thank me for this. If I didn't do it, they'd have to chop your legs off. You'd really be screaming then."

What is this, a Civil War field hospital? Next time, I say chop away, General Sherman.

Tweet Thought @timhawkinscomic
Yesterday I did a kids' workout and I am really feeling it in my head, shoulders, knees, and toes.

Tweet Thought @timhawkinscomic
Flyswatters should be called buzz kills.

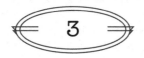

NOAH'S ARK

There is so much about living a life of faith that people have the wrong ideas about. I think they picture the average Christian man as some stick-in-the-mud, uneducated, ultraconservative know-it-all who has never experienced a moment of actual fun in his whole life. Which is patently false—I was educated. But let's be honest, there are weirdos on all sides of the spectrum, both religious and non-religious. I choose to be a weirdo of the Christian persuasion because I have actually met Jesus—and it turns out he likes me.

But people should not act like Christians own the patent on weirdness. There's a Greek word for that: *bulldookie*. Weirdness does not discriminate between the religious and non-religious. John the Baptist was a weird dude. He lived out in the desert by himself. He wore a camel-hair suit with a leather belt. He ate locusts and honey for his food. Come to think of it, this sounds exactly like a fashion statement Lady Gaga would make.

The red carpet teems with paparazzi as the endless flashes of their cameras illuminate the priceless collective wardrobe of Hollywood's elite. Security is tight and only those with the proper celebrity or press credentials can get close to the superstars. "Gaga! Gaga! Who are you wearing this year?"

"Wehhll, the dress is pure Palestinian camel fur by Juan Baptista—it's a far cry in the wilderness from normal. The belt is rich Corinthian leather. Second Corinthian leather, actually. I know, it's totes fierce."

"And tell us about that interesting headpiece?"

"It's pretty amazing, really. It's an elaborate insect wing crafted out of the dried carcasses of actual Egyptian locusts. It's representative of the inner struggle we each feel each day when the sun comes up—I call it Cicadian Rhythm. I've been on a strict locust-honey diet for the past few months and I've never felt better. Now if you'll excuse me, it's almost midnight and soon my giant egg carriage will turn back into a living room beanbag—I will transform back into a normal human being."

My point is that weirdness comes in all shapes and sizes—because every one of us is weird in our own unique way. As Lady Gaga demonstrates, some people's weird ways are just more obvious than others, but I've seen plenty of Christian Gagas out there in my many travels—homeschoolers, you know who you are. You can't hide your full faces under those self-knitted turtlenecks.

None of us should run from faith over the fear of being weird—that's part of the fun. God did not make us to be normal. He made us to be supernatural—and supernatural is not going to look like natural, what with the "super" being added to it and whatnot. The Bible doesn't say God came that we might live more normally, but more abundantly. So it's okay to be abundantly abnormal. I'm not a theologian per se, but I think this makes sense.

Another misconception about faith is that the Bible is a boring book. Honestly, such a statement is much more an indictment that the person saying it has never actually read the Bible than it is of the Bible itself. Eternal blackness suddenly hand-spun like Play-Doh into a universe and the earth as we know it. Naked people walk around in the woods eating fruit and having conversations with snakes. Man-made towers reach into the skies and a global flood covers every square inch of the earth. A laughing nonagenarian gives birth to a baby and a dude is so hairy that a blind guy can't tell him apart from a goat—that joke tells itself. And all that is just in the first book of the Bible.

This book is far from boring. It is full of strange people who did strange and incredible things in their journeys of faith. That's why I read the Bible every day—I am a strange dude walking my own journey of faith with some other like-minded abnormal types.

I love the Bible. I heard a pastor once say that the best version of the Bible is the one you will read. I love that there are various translations of the original languages of the text that help me see all the prisms of perspective within the light of truth. I really love *The Message* Bible. Now *that* is a laid-back Bible. When I was a kid, some guy came out with *The Living Bible*—it was the first paraphrased version of Scripture ever released. Some people got pretty upset about the whole thing, but let me tell you, *The Living Bible* has nothing on *The Message* Bible.

The other day I sat down to read a chapter and I was like, "What is this? The recipe for Rice Krispies treats? Seriously? That's in the Bible?" I turned a few more pages only to discover that the part of Joseph was being played by Johnny Depp. This is awesome. In the New Testament, or as *The Message* Bible calls it, "The Holy After-Party," Jesus changes the water into wine coolers. Amazing. That speaks to me right where I am. They've got to be leaving some stuff out. It's like, "Genesis 1: God made some stuff. Genesis 2." Wait . . . what?

I've noticed that this trend of modernizing how we express our faith has bled over into the way pastors are delivering their sermons. Many pastors have adopted the practice of preaching in series. Twelve-part series. Eighteen-part series. Ninety-part series. Even though there should be, there are no limits.

"How's that *Star Wars*–themed sermon series going?"

"Oh, you mean, 'No Darth, *I'm* His Father'?"

"Yeah."

"Pretty good. But we can't seem to get out of the book of Luke."

"What week in the series are you in?"

"Hmm, do you know how to read scientific notation?"

But no sermon series is complete without a catchy title. You know, something all those who drive by the church marquee will take their eyes off the road to read. Something like, "Content or Discontent: Which Tent Do You Live In?" I see what you did there, Captain Clever.

The really "in" way to brand a series these days is to borrow a name from a popular or recently popular television show—thank God for On Demand. For example, a pastor could speak on seeking direction in confusing situations and call it "Lost." He could speak about anxiety in the daily hullabaloo of life and entitle it "Fear Factor."

I would love to see a church use the "Survivor" concept for a sermon series. Now that would be fun. Every week, a staff member would get voted off. I would show up every week for that. "I hope it's Pastor Steve . . . I hope it's Pastor Steve. Yes! Steve's off! Give him a coconut. He's gone!"

Recently, I encountered one of the more ridiculous titles for a sermon series I have ever heard. And that is saying something. The pastor was like, "All right y'all, I'm so excited about this series we're starting next week. You might want to bring friends because it's going to be real good."

The congregation instinctively moved forward to the edge of their seats as they collectively sensed an energetic anticipation building from the stage. "Lay it on us laypeople, pastor!"

The pastor continued, "Now y'all, I was thinking the other day . . . We all love Twinkies. Twinkies are delicious. But we don't all eat Twinkies the same way. No sir, we do not. Some people break their Twinkies in half. Some shave off the top. Some people drill a hole in them and squeeze out the good stuff. Some people go full commando and shove it straight in their mouths."

I don't know about you, but in my day, we had a different definition of "going commando." I'm just saying.

Pastor Creampuff continued, "So join me next week for the first installment of a forty-eight-part series entitled 'How to Be a Twinkie in a Ding-Dong World.' That's right. Bring your *Message* Bibles. It's going to be anointed!"

Despite the various expressions of those who speak about it, I really do love the Bible. However, I must acknowledge that it can be pretty intense. It seems like people these days sometimes try to retool the Bible into a nice little family-friendly package with a bow on top.

Sure, there's definitely some beautiful stuff in there, but there are also some things that we must admit are more dysfunctionally family friendly. Think about it. There's a reason you don't see certain biblical illustrations in the Precious Moments Bible. "See Cain pummeling Abel with that sharpened goat's horn? How precious!"

That's why I will never understand parents who paint Noah's ark on their little kids' bedroom walls. Honestly, it just doesn't make sense. Noah's ark is a great story, but don't you think it is just a bit "out there" for pastels?

"Daddy, what are you doing?"

"I'm painting Noah's ark on the wall, Sweetheart. It's my favorite Bible story."

"Yay! Will you tell the story to me, Daddy?"

"Sure. Sit up here on my lap. Now, Noah's ark is the one where God sends a worldwide flood to kill every living thing. All the people on the earth, from the youngest to the oldest, died vicious, gruesome deaths by drowning as they desperately clawed the outside of the boat God told Noah to build. Honey, why are you trembling?"

"Daddy, I'm scared!"

"Ah, you'll be fine. Now, grab a brush and paint some screaming people on that rock over there. It's going to be great. Hey, first go look in your baby sister's room—I painted the stoning of Stephen. You're going to love it."

"Are those birds, Daddy?"

"No, those are glow-in-the-dark locusts coming to *get you* when the lights go out."

Nothing like laying a strong biblical foundation for the kids.

Tweet Thought @timhawkinscomic

This is the church

This is the steeple

Open the door

And see all the people

Completely bald with no faces

Tweet Thought @timhawkinscomic

What I know about hell: 1. Has a lake of fire 2. Has weeping and gnashing of teeth 3. You get there by hand basket

ROLLER COASTER

I love being married. I know it sounds cliché, but marriage is a lot like a roller coaster. Or an airplane. Or possibly an episode of *Rin Tin Tin*. Or what the heck, a Brazilian steak house. You know, the ones where they bring out the food to you skewered on swords and daggers and brass knuckles and whatnot? Our steak house is in the bad part of town. But mostly, marriage is like a roller coaster.

I remember what it was like after being married for only three months. The roller coaster is fresh out of the gate, and you both are filled with wild butterflies. You are in the front seat. You feel the metal metronome of CHK-CHK-CHK-CHK-CHK beneath you as the coaster makes its initial ascent. It's easy. Exciting. Thrilling. CHK-CHK-CHK-CHK-CHK. You've got your teddy bear and your sixty-four-ounce cup of Coke. You've got your arm around your sweetheart as you inch close to the first crest. CHK-CHK-CHK-CHK-CHK. "This ain't so bad, is it, sugar booger?" you ask with a nervous smile, trying to look cool. I mean, you're the man, right? CHK-CHK-CHK-CHK-CHK. Nope. Not so bad at all. Then you reach the very top and a little bit of anxiety begins to set in. You realize there's no lid on your Coke and all that excitement from the climb has built up in your bladder. CHK-CHK-CHK-CHK-CHK. Even though this is no Flume Zoom, this is going to be a wet and wild ride. "It's coming, shnookems. Buckle up, patootie. *Aaaahhhh!*"

I do not want to be misunderstood concerning my imaginary hill. I do not mean that the ride is bad. Quite the contrary, marriage is great. I just mean that it changes more than people know when they first pull down the locking mechanism and secure themselves in the plastic seat next to their spouse, which is about the most unromantic way I can think of to describe the wedding. Just call me Nicholas Sparks.

For the dude who has only been married for two months, things are good. Real good. You wake up early to go to work. Get showered and dressed. Stand at the door to leave your room and glance back into your bed where your gorgeous bride is still sleeping in one of your old shirts. She rolls over and brushes her messy hair from her eyes and reaches out toward you in an inviting gesture. With a sleepy, sexy voice she whispers, "Stay . . . just stay." And whether you stay or leave, your woman has seared an image of her unfailing beauty upon your cerebral cortex, no doubt gracing your thoughts with the vision of bliss that awaits you at home after work.

But the CHK-CHK-CHK-CHK-CHK continues. And faster than you anticipate.

A few years later, you wake up to a similar situation. Time to get dressed and head off to work. As you look back at the bed where your wife is sleeping in her parka and electric orthopedic socks, instead of two arms beckoning you to rejoin her in the warmth of the covers, she stretches out a single pointed finger in your general direction. Her voice is low and steady. Barely audible, yet unimaginably loud at the same time. "It's trash day. Let the dog out. Turn out the light." Then she curls up under the blanket just before saying, "You're not going to wear that, are you? Ugh."

Yep. The sweet twisted metal of the marriage coaster has now dubbed you the poster boy for *What Not to Wear*. Congratulations on your success.

When you're first married, you love nothing more than to share each other's food at restaurants. You get a piece of cake after dinner and your wife looks at you with that sexy smirk. "Can I have a bite?"

"Anything for you, my darling." And then you proceed to put the best bite you can find from your cake onto a fork and feed it to her across the table.

But when you've been married for a few years, this same scenario creates justifiable grounds for throwing an elbow. "Here's the deal, honey: I ordered this piece of cheesecake because I wanted this piece of cheesecake. Try to remember back to a minute and a half ago when you did not want a piece of cheesecake. Remember that, dear? But now you want cheesecake."

"I only want a little bite. I'm your wife. Is one tiny piece of cheesecake so much to ask?"

The roller coaster is at full speed and right now, you'd fight Hulk Hogan for that slice of sugary sweetness. "See, that's frustrating because I showed you the menu when the waiter was here at our table. I looked you in the eyes and plainly asked, 'You want cheesecake?' I was very clear. So were you. You said no. I don't see where the confusion is coming from."

"Is that really how you're going to be—and on our anniversary?"

"Look, I got a cheesecake hole in my stomach and half a piece is not going to fill it."

Yes, my married friend. The rules of marriage have changed and you are squarely secured in one of the upside-down loops. They don't warn you in your wedding vows about the G-force challenges that are to come. That's not very romantic. "For richer or poorer. In sickness and in health. At four Gs when you selfishly demand a portion of my cheesecake . . ." The next wedding I am involved in, I am going to plead with the couple to add this language to their ceremony, for no truer or more poetic words of commitment have ever been uttered.

When you're first married, you probably watch each other sleep all the time. She lies there with her head propped up on her hand just gazing at you in your restful state. She thinks to herself, *Oh, look at him. Oh my goodness, he's just so . . . so beautiful when he sleeps. I wonder what he's dreaming about? What am I saying? It's me.* Then she takes a picture and posts it to Facebook with a hundred emoticon hearts behind it. The caption reads, "Where my sweetest dreams lie."

Fast-forward a few years; things change a bit. I woke up from a nap the other day and my wife was just standing there staring at me. I thought it best to just ask her, "Honey, what's wrong?"

Her face bore the weight of confusion and alarm. "I don't remember marrying that face."

Wow, darling. Why don't you just take me to the pound? You might as well call me Chewbacca and throw me a sandwich into the dog bowl. I'm not a monster. "What happened to your nose, Voldemort?"

But there are things one can do to steady the roller coaster of marriage. Obviously, I can only speak from the male perspective, but if I could go back in time and advise the younger married version of myself, I would tell that handsome devil that we must continue to learn. Just learn what she wants. It's real simple. Learn the little things. Little details, Tim. Just little things.

For example, when you go to Starbucks, learn her drink. If you learn what she likes to drink there, you can manage anything else that comes in marriage. Know her drink and it'll blow her mind. No offense intended, but women are very complicated when it comes to these kinds of things—or any kind of thing, I suppose. So you must focus.

Yes, I know that men make easy, simple, and humanly reasonable orders when they go through Starbucks. "Yeah, give me a Venti coffee with cream," I ask the barista quite efficiently. Done and done with time left to evaluate all the reasons and conclude with a harsh judgment the fact that the bottled water by the register costs seventy-five dollars. Where did they dig the well for that stuff—the moon? Then I turn to my wife and begin the proceedings. "Honey, what do you want?"

"Okay, here's what I want. I want a tall skinny sugar-free decaf soy vanilla latte, extra hot, whipped cream, double-sleeve no cup." The life force has now drained from my body. I slowly rotate my empty, yet terrified gaze from my wife to the sweet barista and ask her softly, but urgently, "Please tell me you got that. Please?"

If I were to heed my own time-travel wisdom, then I would have already known how to order this ridiculously long and unnecessarily complicated drink order. You know it's too long when there isn't enough room on the paper cup to write the order. "Hey, we ran out of Sharpie juice again. That lady standing with the funny-looking dude just ordered a tall espresso novella."

But yea, I say, such wisdom doth elude me. I have grown too old and too forgetful to memorize the whipped-cream whims of my wife's Starbucks manifesto. Before the green-aproned woman behind the counter, who has given up on repeating back my wife's order, loses consciousness from repeatedly sniffing the uncapped end of the empty Sharpie, I pipe in with, "I'd like to change my order to a large whiskey. Just a large cup of whiskey, because I'm going to drive away and head for the nearest cliff. I don't want it to hurt so bad."

Oh, and a blueberry scone.

But it's not just drink orders I need to study. It would have behooved me early on to study the nuances of what makes my wife comfortable. I hypothesize that each human on the planet is born with a predetermined number that defines their maximum desired level of comfort. The Sleep Number mattress people have stumbled upon a limited understanding of this bedrock truth, but they are still far away from the target. They may help people find their Sleep Number, but any new husband must know that his beautiful new bride has another number essential to her long-term happiness. I call it her Pillow Potential.

Tragically, many women will live their whole lives and never discover that the source of their discontentment is not what they think. It is not because he won't pick up his dirty socks and deposit them in the hamper. Neither is it the fact that his morning breath reeks of camel bile. No, actually her uneasiness could be easily remedied with the addition of more soft head supports—that is to say, pillows. Ironically, adding more down brings a marriage up. Pillow Potential is the key.

When I was first married, I thought all we needed was two pillows on the bed. Obviously, that is not nearly enough. I was shooting way too low. I suppose I was thinking like a human instead of thinking like a woman. But I adjusted and listened to her unspoken needs. Now, we have exactly thirty-seven pillows on our bed and she couldn't be happier.

We don't even need a mattress anymore. We just have pillows stacked four deep creeping toward the center from the four corners of the box springs. Is it practical? Come on, is that really a fair question for marriage? If I had wanted practical, I would have just bought a dog or saved money. My wife's Pillow Potential, as it has played out in our home, may not be the most pragmatic way for me to sleep every night—you know, almost suffocating to death as the piles of pillows take up arms around me. Some mornings, I wake up and I can't even recall where I am. I think it's all the memory foam. But if my wife is happy, then it is worth every stray feather.

So husbands everywhere have some decisions to make. Are we willing to endure these mounds of pillows in our beds every night for the sake of love? When we wake up at 2:00 a.m. and we need to get out of bed to get a drink, we must each ask ourselves the question, "Do I have the strength to climb Mt. Pillowmanjaro?"

I'm confident you will make the right decision. Just grab your harness and carabiner and rappel down that bad boy straight into marital bliss. You, my friend, are taking charge of the roller coaster of marriage. *Ricola!*

Tweet Thought @timhawkinscomic

In most arguments between a man and a woman, the man feels like he's on the same page. He just doesn't know how to read.

Tweet Thought @timhawkinscomic

Every time I'm driving on a bumpy road without a stopper in my Starbucks cup, I totes relate to the early settlers.

5

SUPERNANNY

I think anyone who has children could use a little help. I don't need health care from the government. I want a nanny. In fact, I want the Supernanny. This woman is a miracle worker and she does it with such style. Such sophistication. Such patience. Yep, the Supernanny would change the Hawkins household forever. Since she is from England, we would have to actually learn how to speak English, but methinks 'twould be worth the effort.

Supernanny is the best show ever. This British nanny flies across the Atlantic on a humanitarian crusade to help these demonic kids from America. And when I say demonic, I wish I were exaggerating. I don't know what description they use in the casting call for this show, but I imagine that it goes something like this. "Wanted: real people for popular reality show on parenting. We need young children who won't hesitate to rip their own parents' faces off when asked to pick up their rooms. They must also be willing to start chemical fires in the family room, punch holes in the drywall with their foreheads, stab their siblings with sharp kitchen utensils, use profanity with the proficiency of a thirty-year sailor with a meth addiction, and have necks that unhinge and rotate their heads a full three hundred and sixty degrees. Please send video."

And somewhere out there, some poor mother reading the ad in the newspaper looks up at her husband and says, "Honey, Jimmy's going to be a star! Bring my quiver of Ritalin darts and the circus cage trailer. We're going to that casting call!"

These children are in absolute beast mode. While some kids

are talking too loudly or refusing to share their stuffed bunny with a neighbor, these kids are sneaking brass knuckles into the sandbox and making FBI watch lists. For real. It's no wonder these parents are ready to throw in the towel—or douse the towel in chloroform.

But Supernanny never loses her cool. In her calm and reassuring British accent, she gently chides the young terrorist. "No, Thomas. No, we don't do that, Thomas . . ." Accent or not, somehow those few little no-nos seem to retilt the axis of the evil earth these crazed tykes inhabit.

"What do you mean 'what did I do?' You just knocked your mother out cold with a pot. That's not what we do. We don't do that. I'm very disappointed, Thomas. I'm going to have to get harsh. You heard me, hhhhaurssh. I hate to do this to you, but go sit on the naughty mat. You heard me—the naughty mat!"

And inexplicably, Thomas puts down the flamethrower and starts profusely crying tears of remorse. Remorse, I say! Up to this point in his short yet eventful little life, Thomas has only felt a few emotions. Anger. Jealousy. The occasional rage manifested by long tantrums and hyper-destructive behavior. But remorse? Negative, Ghost Rider. Like a little anti-patriot, the only thing Thomas has regretted is that his little brother has but one life to give. But somehow, Thomas is now crying because he has to sit on a mat—a mat he would have set ablaze only a few days before Supernanny's arrival.

Supernanny motions for the parents to come out from hiding behind the armoire. Like frightened deer approaching a bloodthirsty grizzly, they emerge from their position with tattered clothes and hair matted with the fresh blood of their previously sustained flesh wounds. The trembling lips of the mother mime to Supernanny three words: "Is it safe?"

"Yes. Yes, it is," Supernanny replies with a confident assurance the parents have never experienced. "Thomas is ready to be a good little boy now. Isn't that right, Thomas?" Thomas, still seated and sniffling on the naughty mat, now clothed and in his right mind, gently nods his head affirmatively. Like a wild stallion on the open range, he has been broken. Domesticated. Tamed. And as the family begins to rebuild the shattered wreckage of their lives, the credits start rolling down the screen. Another desperate household is changed thanks to the efforts of the Supernanny and her magical floor mat.

I'm sitting at home thinking that there's got to be more to it. Is Thomas sitting on the mat while you go find something to beat him with? Because I do not know how everyone else was raised, but when I was growing up, there were no "naughty mats" in our home—well, except when my friend Matt would come over. But that's different.

If I was the Supernanny one week, you might want to tune in because that would be an entirely different show. "Thomas, get in the car. No, I'm not putting you on the naughty mat. I'm going to drive you off a naughty cliff. That's right. Get in the car. You don't need shoes; you're not coming back. We're going to meet Jesus!"

If Supernanny is a superhero, then my mom was like Lex Luther. When I would run amuck like Thomas, Mom was not calling anyone to come to her aid. No, it was me who would need the aid. And the crazy part was that all she had to do was tell me what she was going to do to me. She had a rare gift of expressiveness when getting her point across.

"I am going to beat the snot out of you! You hear me? I'mma beat the snot . . . outta you! I'mma hit your head so hard, snot's gonna fly outta the front of your skull. It's gonna be awesome!"

Yes, she was a pretty big fan of snot and all the colorful possibilities it presented. So much so, when she was extremely mad, she would threaten to beat the living snot out of me. "I'mma beat the livin' snot outta you. Your snot's gonna have a respiratory system when I beat it outta your head!"

Oh let me tell you, she was detailed. "I'm gonna spin your head off like the lid off a pickle jar! I'm gonna take my leather belt with my name on it and I'm gonna beat you and brand you at the same time!"

Sure, I would occasionally attempt one of those moves like the demon children on *Supernanny* try to pull. I would say something hurtful and hope it would make her feel guilty—you know, gain the emotional upper hand. "Mommy, you're the worst mommy in the world!" Ooh, that was a low blow, something sure to bring tears to the eyes of a tenderhearted maternal caregiver.

My mom? She didn't miss a beat, if you know what I mean. "No, I took second last year. I'm going for first this year!" I guess she took the imaginary rating system more seriously than I first thought. One time she spanked me for something I didn't even do. But did she apologize? Ha! "That's for something you'll do later!" What is this, Mom? Do I have a spank account? I think you're writing checks my butt can't cash, old lady.

My mom got the job done with unrivaled speed, efficiency, and creativity. All joking aside, she was the sweetest and most loving mother on the planet, but you can bet your sweet bippy that she had no need for naughty mats. And thus we had no need for the Supernanny.

Tweet Thought @timhawkinscomic
I try to live every day as if it were my first. So I take a lot of long naps and cry a lot till someone brings me milk.

Tweet Thought @timhawkinscomic
My parents taught me the difference between a "come to Jesus" meeting and a "go to meet Jesus" meeting.

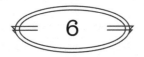

6

WRISTBAND CHEAT SHEET

I love Texas. I don't actually live there anymore, but the state will always have a place in my heart. Maybe that's why, win or lose, I am a Dallas Cowboys fan. Truth is, there's usually more losing involved these days than winning. Brings a single tear to my eye. I'm just kidding. Everyone knows Cowboys fans don't have any tears left. Or hope. Or souls, for that matter.

I am a fan of America's team, though, if we can still call them that. The Cowboys do look a lot like America these days. Both have stars in their logos (or flags). Both like huge flat screens for game watching. Both have leaders who spend way too much and win way too little. But just like my patriotism, my fanhood is fully intact. Boo all you want, but this cowboy is a . . . well, a Cowboy.

I get so excited about the games that sometimes I fumble the remote control just seeing quarterback Tony Romo take the field. Imitation is the highest form of flattery. Seriously, though, I do love watching NFL quarterbacks lead their teams down the field of play. Such poise. Such leadership. Such huge wristbands on their arms.

Honestly, I never knew what those wristbands were all about. Shopping lists? Shakespearean poetry? Pictures of their moms to bring them comfort just before they are clobbered by four-hundred-pound linemen? Nope. I found out they are the plays.

The plays? Seriously? These guys have cheat sheets strapped to their wrists? I was appalled, to say the least. I guess I expect more from a bunch of strangers I've never met. Hey Captain, how much money do you make—like ten billion dollars a year? I'm thinking maybe you could take some time to *learn the plays*.

These guys get like six months off every off-season. If I had that kind of time off, I think I could learn almost anything no matter how absolutely impossible it was. The study guide for the bar exam. An entire Spanish dictionary. My wife's drink order at Starbucks. You know, anything.

What kinds of ridiculous things are these guys doing with their time off anyway? Playing Xbox? Eating endless boxes of Swedish Fish? Trying to learn their wife's drink order at Starbucks?

Maybe there's more to the story of the mysterious wristband. Much more indeed. Perhaps the wristband cheat sheet contains more than just reminders of the plays. Maybe it is the literal linchpin of a quarterback's ability to do anything in football—like a secret key that, if removed, would leave him unable to perform even the most menial of tasks. It would render him more like, well, me. Oh, the humanity.

If this were the case, then these super-juiced athletes would be so dependent on said cheat sheets that perhaps even I could see the need to use them during games on Sundays. The cheat sheet is the jelly to their peanut butter. The tool belt to their Batman costume. The Wilson to their Tom Hanks.

Yet I can't help but think about the first day in training camp when Romo strapped on his secret-weapon cheat-sheet wristband and began doing its evil bidding. He probably tightened his chinstrap and stepped up behind that offensive line ready to see his professional career take off. "Hall of Fame, here I come."

Then the wristband began its wild, diabolical demands. "Okay, step one. To receive ball, place hands gently under . . ." The young quarterback slowly raised his gaze to behold the "south end zone" of a three-hundred-pound plumber-cracked center bent over in front of him ready to hike the ball. "I'm not doing that! Oh, come on!" He finagled his hands in various positions near the offended area, but he just couldn't find a way to make it work. "Darn you, cruel wristband! There must be another way. Can he not just throw it over his shoulder or something? I need some hand sanitizer over here. Let's do the shotgun thing and I'll just do this with my leg and you can just fling it to me."

Come on. A cheat sheet? You don't see other professional athletes using cheat sheets. NASCAR driver looks down at his wrist. "Okay, up ahead turn left. What's next? Okay, another left. I can do that. Oh, another left. I think I'm beginning to see a pattern forming." So I guess I'm not real sure why these quarterbacks think they don't have to study like the rest of the sporting world.

Football in America is like anything else that Americans do when given control. If a little is good, then a lot is better, right? So when it comes to watching football, one game is sufficient, but now we can watch every game at the same time. Yes, Dorothy, we did it. We call it the NFL Red Zone channel.

NFL Red Zone is relentless. It's every game, at the same time, on the same channel. Every time a team is about to score they switch over to that game. It's an onslaught of action, and it's just too much. I'm paying eighty bucks a month for an anxiety attack.

I need an escape. So, after watching Red Zone for an hour, I have to turn over to Bob Ross, the painting guy on PBS. He gently beckons me, "Come, my friend. Stay awhile. Watch me paint a happy tree. Take a nap in my afro."

Tweet Thought @timhawkinscomic
Just throw your hands in the air.
And wave 'em like you just don't care.
And that should get you out of jury duty.

Tweet Thought @timhawkinscomic
Did P90X today. That's where you play 90 minutes of Xbox.

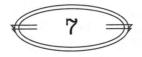

COLONOSCOPY

There are parts of being forty that I did not anticipate. I thought it was all about being older. Wiser. Richer.

My doctor ruined those notions. Apparently forty only grants my doctor more rights to inflict great amounts of pain on the most sensitive and private parts of my aging body—and then to charge me an arm and a leg for his service. I wish, though, he was dealing only with my arms and legs.

I wrote an original song to commemorate the horror of my doctor's insistence on excellence in his diabolical orifice witch hunt. This way, more people can join in the fun.

COLONOSCOPY

You have some lovely children and a lovely wife
You have a lovely bank account and had a healthy life
But you knew the day was coming
It was always meant to be
Your doctor says, "It's time to have a colonoscopy."

Oh colon, colon, colonoscopy
A wonderful procedure as everyone can see
Your number's up, it's time to take one for the team
It's right there on the schedule, colonoscopy

There is some preparation that you should know about
You have to drink this fluid that will surely clean you out
They'll take a certain instrument to take a look inside
And honestly I'll tell you it can be a bumpy ride

Oh colon, colon, colonoscopy
A wonderful procedure to help prevent disease
Stay close to a bathroom and careful when you sneeze
You can't get away from colonoscopies

It's not a lot of pleasure, it's not a lot of fun
But now you're turning forty, so you know it must be done
It's not an ordinary typical exam
You lie down on a table and then, "THANK you, ma'am."

Oh colon, colon, colonoscopy
A wonderful procedure I'm sure you will agree
Never underestimate how thorough they will be
It's time to take your medicine, colonoscopy

Tweet Thought @timhawkinscomic
I call McDonald's "Mickey D's" and I call Buffalo Wild Wings
"B Dubs" and I call Taco Bell "Voldemort's Colon."

Tweet Thought @timhawkinscomic
I'm coming out with a new scent. And now it's gone.

A HOMESCHOOL FAMILY

I love lazy mornings. On this one in particular, the sunrise was gently cast with a delicate orange hue as low-hanging clouds smattered a kaleidoscope of colors from heaven's palette upon the canvas of the dawning sky. They must have been divine watercolors because soon they gave way to the gentle pitter-patter of raindrops on my roof. An atmospheric lullaby. An angelic condensation.

I liked it goodly.

As I dozed beneath the blanket of the delightful melody, I became increasingly aware that the gentle pitter-patter was becoming less and less gentle. In fact, it was beginning to sound more like a stampede. Not a normal stampede with cattle, mind you. No, cows would be welcome company compared to these creatures, which is the first time I have imagined a scenario in which cattle would be welcome company anywhere, much less my home. I like cows in my house like I like my steaks: rare.

But these sounds were not coming from my roof at all. They were coming from inside my house—emanating from the stomping feet of a smaller breed of beast. More focused. More vicious. And they were moving up the stairs. Toward my room.

Bam! Like a water blast from a broken hydrant, two Lords of the Flies burst through our door and began pouncing upon my midsection, which apparently is the most instinctive action of this barbaric species. They must huddle together, overdosing on Go-Gurts, before an invasion and communicate to each other in prehistoric grunts and clicking noises, "Okay Crag, we get in, you find man in room. Jump straight on crotch. Attack!"

Still stubbornly bent on clinging to my sleep until the bitter end (which was near), for a split second I actually did not remember what these filthy little intruders were. Then one of them spoke. Like Charlton Heston in *Planet of the Apes*, I gasped, "It can *talk*!" But even more alarming was what it said—a word that violently wrangled me back into reality as my memory banks were still being viciously primed back to the present via the continual pouncing of the midsection.

"Dad!"

Yep. There it was. The pain of reality. When you are a dad, there are no lazy mornings, only lazy children. Yet somehow, laziness for them does not translate as laziness did for me in college and young adulthood: into sleeping late. They can't do dishes, wipe themselves, or stop tying their shoestrings in knots—and they also can't sleep past 5:45 a.m. Ah, the cruel irony of the universe repaying me for my own childhood angst.

Why am I in this situation called fatherhood in the first place? I mean, I remember very well how it technically happened. There was actually a ribbon-cutting ceremony, if I remember it correctly, and I was presented a key to the city. Anyway, I guess I am more wondering why I have subjected myself to this madness. And to add insult to injury, on this drizzly Tuesday morning most dads out there are carting their young off to a magical wonderland called public school where children are cared for by other adults, granting parents a leisurely seven hours of freedom.

But not I. I'm just getting started. For I am a . . . homeschool dad. (Let it echo in your inner soul with deeply dramatic reverb.)

How did this condition overtake me and apparently with my consent? Was I drugged? Am I drugged now? Am I really asking myself these questions in my own journal as if I could actually get an answer from myself? What other questions could I muse about to myself aimlessly? Have the cows taken over my consciousness?

Focus. I am reminded that in the old days, homeschooling was mostly for those members of society who dwelt out on the fringes. Fairies, hobbits, and the like. Most of the people who were homeschooling their children were either from the extreme right or extreme left wing. You had the families who dressed alike, wearing their jean skirts to the floor and their shirts buttoned to the ceiling. And then you had hippies. So on one end, you had people who made their own soap, and on the other you had people who never used soap. On one end, people who crafted their own ceramic pots. On the other, people who grew their own pot. You know, homeschoolers.

I'm no idiot. Well, mostly. I know this is what most people still think when they find out we are homeschoolers. I see the judgmental stares of the heartless masses tearing us apart mental limb by mental limb. We're not animals. Well, except for our children, I suppose. Please refer to previous section about my children being animals.

The biggest criticism I hear on homeschooling is that my kids won't get proper socialization. But come on, we all remember what school was like. What did we get in trouble for the most? Socializing. And then they put us out in the hall by ourselves, which is just like homeschooling. Take that, logic. I also hear this one: if you don't send your children to public school, they won't be like their peers. I don't want my kids to be like their peers. I want them to be like me. Which, now that I think about it, might be the worst commercial ever devised for homeschooling.

Look, I get it. Homeschooling is not for everybody. In fact, I'm not even sure it is for me. Just last year, I decided to teach math to my kids for the semester. I will never forget the letter I received in the mail at the end of our homeschool coursework. It systematically laid out each of our children's grades in their various areas of study. Everything looked great, except for one subject: math. Across the board, they were all failing. Tucked inside the letter was a pink slip. I got fired . . . by my wife. Sure it stings a bit, but what are you going to do? She's the boss. And she holds the key to the city.

I now consider it a strange promotion. I have been elevated to the position of school principal—or more accurately, evil principal—complete with the gentle stroking of an equally evil cat. It is a remote position with offices headquartered at our local Starbucks. I drink lattes and wait for my wife to call when the kids need discipline or when my debit card is needed for homeschool fairs. I know my role. And if you don't know what a homeschool fair is, just picture a regular fair without any cool people for which you pay one hundred bucks to walk around and realize what a failure you are as a father because you haven't taught your own little nonsocialized math morons anything about ceramics and soap making. I ended the day sitting on the concrete steps outside the convention center crying and sucking my thumb.

But all in all, we are just like other people in society. Besides the class location and the illiteracy, we are pretty normal. (Really, I don't have a problem with public school. It's just too early, and I don't want to get up and take them.) The most glaring difference between our lives and the lives of families who send their kids to public school? The bumper stickers. Their stickers read, "My Son Is an Honor Student at Heritage Academy." Our bumper reads, "Our Kids Are Homeschooled . . . and We Have No Idea How They Are Doing."

Last week, someone asked me what grade my kid was in. Awkward. I leaned down and quietly whispered to my son, "How old are you?"

"Nine," he whispered back.

"Ninth grade. He's in the ninth grade."

I mean, how do you actually determine something like that in our situation? Sure he can recite the Greek alphabet and use the quadratic equation to solve math problems, but he still jams bars of soap down the toilet. Oh tiny mathematician, heal thyself. I shouldn't get too worked up about it. Latex gloves are pretty cheap. Cognitive and educational evaluations are enigmatic in our situation, to say the least. It is complex. "Hey, make Daddy some breakfast and I'll give you extra credit for home ec."

I wonder if other homeschoolers are like mine. I do encounter quite a few of them out there in the wild. I'm so proud of them when they have the courage to come to my shows. I always have them raise their hands so I can publicly honor them with the question, "What's it like being outside?" They love that stuff. And in all seriousness, being outside the mother ship must be a lot to take in. "A whole new world . . ." Eat it, Aladdin.

And they are always so studious, bringing their journals and taking notes with the homemade quill pens they made from chicken feathers. You've got to remember that to homeschoolers, it is not a comedy show—it's a field trip. I don't know, maybe I should write a song about this stuff for my show. It has so profoundly impacted me. It could work. Maybe people would even want to hear me sing it on YouTube.

Nah, that's a dumb idea. Get it together, Timbo. At any rate, I'm thinking something like this to the tune of *The Addams Family*. I'll work it out later.

Some people say we're goofy
Mysterious and spooky
Our neighbors think we're kooky
A homeschool family

We drive a white conversion
We learn about the Persians
Our six-year-old's a surgeon
A homeschool family

We learn about creation
And classic education
We're sponsoring a Haitian
A homeschool family

The parents are the tutors
We build our own computers
We never go to Hooters
A homeschool family

Have recess in the foyer
And then we read *Tom Sawyer*
Our nine-year-old's a lawyer
A homeschool family

We never leave our dwelling
Our children are excelling
They're champions at spelling
A homeschool family

Well you can say we're nerdy
And homeschool is absurdy
But we're over by 10:30
A homeschool family

Tweet Thought @timhawkinscomic
Sure, I was homeschooled, but that's neither hear nor their.

Tweet Thought @timhawkinscomic
Another advantage of being a homeschooler is it's easier to find your graduation cap after throwing it in the air.

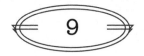

NOOK AND CRANNY

The following is an excerpt from my 1985 journal:

Moms are the *worst*. I just don't get it. I mean, what did I do so wrong? She freaked out on me today—again. Someday I'm going to earn enough money cutting grass to buy a totally cool black Camaro and then I'm outta here faster than Marty McFly in 1955.

I was so mad that I paged my friend Kenny. A 9–1–1 page. I heard back from him an hour later when he could get to a pay phone. I need to get me one of those new rad portable phones—the one in the bag that plugs into your car's cigarette lighter and has that cool antenna riding on your roof, like, seven feet in the air. So modern and convenient.

Kenny and I rode our bikes down to the arcade. I needed a good game of Pac-Man. Video games are great for dudes because we can have deep, heartfelt conversations without the necessity of eye contact. After a few games, we sat down to talk everything out over a New Coke and some Pop Rocks. Dude, those things are magical. I love a candy that shoots out of your mouth and hits your friend in the eye while you're talking to him. And if you're talking to a pretty girl? The original eye candy. Awesome. Pop Rocks aren't candy. They are a science experiment. Just last week we bought a new pet bird and I fed it some Pop Rocks. The next day we went out and got a new bird.

"I just don't understand her!" I said to Kenny. "It's like we aren't even speaking the same language."

Kenny was just finishing tight-rolling the cuffs of his jeans for the eighth time in the last hour. He then adjusted his oversized, sleeveless "Where's the Beef?" workout shirt, cut all the way down to his belt line. "Dude. I know what you mean. Sometimes my mom doesn't understand me either."

"No, dude. I don't think you understand. I mean that she doesn't use real words."

"Oh," said Kenny as he stroked the dual lines shaved in the side of his head. "What did she say?"

I went on to tell him the whole story from earlier that day—a story I knew all too well, for it had happened all too many times. I came home from school like any other day and when I walked in the door, Mom started in on me.

"Timmy! Did you clean your room this morning like I told you to?"

"Um, I think so." I was being serious. It's not like she gave me a lot of detailed instruction. All I knew is that I needed to clean "every nook and cranny." But how was I supposed to know what in the world a "nook" was? Or a cranny, for that matter? I really didn't know.

A few weeks ago, after attempting a room clean, I yelled, "Hey, *Mom.* Is my nook dirtier than my cranny?" She inspected. "Well, your nook is fine, but your cranny is filthy. It's embarrassing. You have the filthiest cranny in the neighborhood. Have you seen the Thompson kids' crannies? Clean as a whistle. If you had half the cranny that Billy Thompson has . . ."

But back to my story to Kenny. I told him that I honestly did remember straightening things up before I left. You know, I picked up all the striped socks on the floor and put away the tubes of hair gel on the vanity. I had even remembered to turn off VH1 on the television after adjusting the rabbit ears.

"Do you call this clean?" That was simply a warm-up pitch. I could tell she was ready to bring the heat.

"Mom . . ."

And that was all I said. The ticking time bomb that was my mother suddenly exploded and I was the target.

"Don't mom me! How dare you mom me like that!"

Then I poured my heart out to Kenny. What in the world was

she talking about? Is it really possible to "mom" someone? And if said "momming" is indeed a thing, when exactly does it occur? Which random "mom" constitutes a legitimate "momming," and which ones are considered just harmless "mom-bys"?

The questions raced through my mind like Spy Hunter, but I didn't have time to vocalize them. "The momming stops now, smart aleck. Go to your room."

So I did. I walked in to find my brother Todd sitting on my bed. "Dude, what are you doing in my room?"

Todd gave me the same look I was giving him. "Not sure. This is where she sent me for some reason. I think she got us confused again."

Todd rolled his eyes. "What happened this time?"

"I think I 'mommed' mom."

Like Todd and myself, Kenny was dumbfounded. I went on to tell him that this wasn't the only strange vocabulary my mom used. We also were very accustomed to hearing the words, "I won't have it!"

What could that mean? You won't have what . . . a coherent sentence?

Kenny made me feel better, though, because he helped me dream of the day that I will get her back real good. When she throws one of her lines at me, I'm going to be ready. I can hear it now. "Clean up your room. I am not going to say it again."

Crickets chirp in absolute serenity. "Cool. You're not going to say it again. You're finally going to shut your mouth about the whole thing." Once and for all, the room cleaning affair is settled. That will be a golden silence unlike any other. "Hey Mom, are you going to e-mail me or something?"

"Don't mom me! And what in the world is e-mail? I won't have it!"

Tweet Thought @timhawkinscomic
Kids are like sponges. If they get all crusty, hold them under water until they become usable again.

Tweet Thought @timhawkinscomic
I think I'm failing as a parent. The other day I told my son to behave like a man, so he laid on the couch and scratched himself for 15 minutes.

TURQUOISE TOILET

What an incredible life I get to lead. I have the honor of traveling all across this great nation sharing joy and laughter with hundreds of thousands of incredible people. Yep, the old Red, White, and Blue is what I'm all about.

And yes, I do work pretty hard at my job. A lot of people assume that being funny just comes naturally to comedians. Truth is, it is hard work and I haven't always done it well. I've had many other jobs, from waiting tables to driving a grocery delivery truck. But no job has been harder than what I do now. Writing jokes all day is no day at the park. Some days I also go to Starbucks. Hey, Carson. Where's my Venti? I'm losing inspiration over here.

But today I was reminded that though my job is tough, there is a person I know and love who has it much rougher than me: my wife. After twentyish years of marriage, she continues to be my biggest hero in this world. I tell her all the time. So you'd think I wouldn't have to learn this one the hard way.

You'd be wrong.

I came in from a three-day trip and my wife was just standing there in the hallway. Taking slow, deliberate breaths. Waiting for me. Possibly concealing a weapon behind her back. I was too far away to tell. I approached her with caution. "Honey, I'm home."

Her expression did not change and somehow without her mouth moving at all, she said, "Yeah, I heard you pulling up."

"Can I have a hug?"

"Mhmm," was her response. Yes, that was the sound she made.

Don't ask me how I know how to spell it. Her eyes were blinking, but not in unison. Somehow the right eye was about a half second off the left. This was bad.

"What's the problem?" I gently prodded.

"You need to take the kids somewhere, and you need to do it now!"

"Okay. Where do you want me to take them?"

"I don't give a rat's salad shooter where you take them. Just get out of here!"

The kids suddenly appeared from behind me, seeking shelter in my shadow. We all slowly began to back away toward the door. "Okay, we're going to leave."

I turned to the kids and whispered, "Get in the car." But they weren't moving fast enough, so I shouted, "Get in the car!"

As we pulled out of the driveway, my wife stood in the doorway watching us. I rolled down the window and said, "We're going to go. We'll be back in . . . June."

So now I was in the car with all four of my kids and I had absolutely no idea where to go. Where does one go to find solace and direction in moments of pain and confusion? It hit me. I took them to Home Depot. I figured we could just look at hammers for a while—you know, let the dust settle around our lives a bit. Shop for chain saws or eat a few nails. Rub Gojo on our bare chests and lay out in the landscaping department with the glass ceiling. Just get away from it all.

But Home Depot was no more the right choice for that particular day than my actual home. It turns out you can't just let your kids run amuck at a home improvement store. I call that false advertisement. Still, you have never really lived until you turn the corner near the plumbing aisle only to behold your youngest son proudly using the display toilet. There's a Kodak moment for you right there. Hey, James Dobson, why don't you focus on my family for a little while, what say you?

The manager was looking right at me. I smiled a little and said,

"Yeah, that's my boy. Should be done in a minute or so. Do y'all take Visa? Okay, that's good."

Just what Daddy wanted—a gently used turquoise toilet.

Tweet Thought @timhawkinscomic
Whenever I want to be left alone, I go to the mall and hold a clipboard.

Tweet Thought @timhawkinscomic
You "Save the earth" people can go ahead and use one square of toilet paper. I'm gonna keep wrapping it around my hand like a beehive.

YOGA PANTS

This may be the most amazing song I have ever written, or it may not be. Let the vagueness intrigue you. Don't doubt me, though. These stanzas are about real life. As real as it gets. No music required—the lyrics will suffice to express the deepest part of my soul.

My wife was out for three days to visit her mom
I was supposed to cook and clean while she was gone
Somehow she never buckles under all the demands
I had to know her secret, I had to understand

Well I thought it might be coffee but that gives her the shakes
It might be soap operas but she says they're too fake
It's not the car she drives or what she puts in her hair
I realized it's got to be something that she wears
Yoga pants, she wears them all day
Yoga pants, at work and at play
Yoga pants, what's all the fuss?
What makes them so special that they keep them from us?
Yoga pants

Well any normal person would leave it alone
But I'm not a normal person and nobody was home
My wife was out of town and the kids were outside
I went into the bedroom and decided I would try . . . her

Yoga pants, so stretchy and thin
Yoga pants, feels like my own skin
I've never done yoga, but these make me want to try

Yoga pants, so soft and so sleek
Yoga pants, feels good on my cheeks
Yoga pants, I'll just say thanks
I don't wear yoga pants . . . I wear Spanx
Yoga pants .

Tweet Thought @timhawkinscomic
"I enjoy your husband's hot pants." —A lady trying to tell my wife that she likes my "Yoga Pants" song.

Tweet Thought @timhawkinscomic
Thanks, North Face, for cutting-edge technology that keeps people warm from their cars to the front door of Starbucks.

HEDGE OF PROTECTION

As a man of faith who spends most of his time traveling to churches, I have become more and more attuned to the irreplaceable value of prayer in one's life. It is such a vital component of spiritual vitality.

Since I grew up in church, I heard all kinds of different prayers all the time—different styles and whatnot. Over the years, I have become somewhat of a student of the little quirks people have when they pray. I am especially fascinated by a few little phrases that I still do not understand to this day.

If I've heard it once, I've heard it a thousand times. "Father, we just pray a hedge of protection around Tim and his family." This one rarely comes unaccompanied by a deeply sweet southern drawl. "Now Timbo, we are praying a hedge of protection around you, buddy. That's right, mmm hmm. Around you and your whole family."

A hedge, huh? I don't mean to complain, but is that really the best you can do? How about praying a thick cement wall with some razor wire on top of that bad boy? A hedge of protection sounds like it is one good pair of clippers away from being removed—and I'm sure the devil's got a pair of those lying around the old Sheol Shed.

But I guess certain church people think a hedge is going to scare the devil away. I can just see a red, pointy-eared wily devil prancing up to my spiritual property line. Creeping in for an attack. But just as he is about to step onto my lawn, he becomes keenly aware that something is not right. And for some reason, I imagine this particular devil with the sophisticatedly British accent of a classic diabolical villain.

"What is this I behold on this lawn of my enemy's perch? Is this greenery? I can't get through that! Father of all lies? Sure. Originator of the fall of man? That was a cinch. Tempter of the nations? Child's play. But a hedge? Now this is serious!" The whole ridiculous imaginary encounter continues to mushroom cloud in my brain as Satan's minions gather round to bemoan the shrubbery's impenetrable might. "My greatest weakness is landscaping. How did they know? Move that bush!" End scene.

Truth be told, I do appreciate prayers in any form, even when hedges are being raised. Hey, prayer is prayer. I'll take as much as people are willing to give—more or less. Sometimes, the "more" can be overwhelming, especially when someone is praying while they are nervous. It is not uncommon for them to say a certain word like *just* just a little too much.

The small group stands in a circle and joins hands as the lead pray-er takes charge at lightning speed, "Lord-I-just-want-to-just-come-to-just-experience-just-we-just-just-just-in-justliness-and-justification . . ."

And I'm thinking to myself, *Just finish the prayer. You're just not ready for this. Start stacking chairs.*

My dad does this when he prays, but in a different way. The whole family gathers around the Thanksgiving table to give thanks for the bounty before us. The hallowed patriarch of our clan slowly pans across the many faces surrounding him. Some young and ruddy with hope. Some etched with the laugh lines of many good years lived. The old man's eyes well up with gratitude as his heart reflects upon times past and the foundations laid before him that have led to this overwhelming moment of blessing.

He calls his precious family to join hands. Tiny fingers grasp wrinkled ones as each generation looks to Dad at the end of the table for guidance and reflection in this most sacred moment. Heads bow and eyes close as the whole family opens its collective heart for a well-articulated prayer to encapsulate the beauty of the spirit everyone is feeling.

Dad sighs in a moment of silence. Finally, he begins to pray with, "Father . . ."

There is a sense of awe in the room. This is going to be rich. Dad continues with yet another, "Father . . ."

One of the young ones looks up with one eye. It's beginning. Again. Dad finally erupts. "Father, we come to you, Father, in the Spirit, Father, you are Father, Father . . . father-father-just-just-father-father-just-just-father-father . . ."

Yep. Dad prays those "father-father" prayers. We don't talk to our friends like that.

"Ed, Ed, come over, Ed, Ed-Ed-Ed-Ed-Ed-Ed-Ed." Ed wouldn't be your friend anymore if you did that. "He keeps saying Ed. My name's Joe!"

Prayer can be a funny thing indeed. But even if we don't repeat certain words like *just* or *father*, we do have some strange phrases we use. The funniest is the way people pray over food. "Lord, bless this food and the hands that have prepared it." The hands that have prepared it? Why not the whole body? Nope. Just the hands.

Sometimes we pray over food and ask God to make up for our bad choices. "Lord, bless this food to the nourishment of our bodies." But sometimes we have to admit, what we are choosing to eat has no nutritional value in any sense of the word. "Lord bless this . . . this bag of Cheetos. And this jumbo Dr. Pepper. Lord, somehow make this nourish us in some way."

As the need for the miraculous surrounding our request grows, so do the intensity and volume of our prayer. "God, I don't know how you're gonna do it, Father, but we just trust in you now. Father, change the molecular structure of this food . . . this complete trash we're about to shove in our gullet. Transform the Cheeto into a carrot stick with fat-free ranch dressing on the way down. Spirit of low carb, reign down on me now! I pray a hedge of protection around my pancreas, Lord. Right now. Intervene!"

All joking aside, though, I suppose any prayer is good. Well, maybe that's not true. I think there are some truly bad prayers out there. The worst prayers? The ones parents pray with their kids at bedtime. No wonder kids don't want to go to sleep.

When I was a kid, my lovely parents would sit on the end of my bed to pray with me. My memory may be tainted a bit due to post-traumatic stress syndrome, but to my best recollection, our prayer time went something like this.

"Now I lay me down to sleep. I pray the Lord my soul . . . to keep."

By this time, sharp devil horns had sprouted out of my dad's forehead as the red lights of his neon eyes cast dancing shadows upon the melting walls. "If I should . . . die. Before I wake. I pray the Lord my soul . . . to take." I lay shivering in both figurative and literal puddles as my parents left the room.

"Sweet dreams. See you in the morning. Maybe. I'd say it's fifty-fifty. I can't guarantee. Oh and don't let the bedbugs bite." And then the parental psychopath would trail off into maniacal laughter. My brother polished off the whole future therapy session by making up his own little psychotic lullabies when they left the room. "Go to sleep. Little creep. Close your big bloodshot eyes. Go to sleep little creep. Or your teddy bear will die."

You know, bedtime prayers.

Tweet Thought @timhawkinscomic
Whenever God closes a door, he opens a window. If the window is locked, then you've obviously done something really bad.

Tweet Thought @timhawkinscomic

Remember, Christians: Let your yes be "yes" and your no be "I'll pray about it."

GOOD ADVICE
TOO LATE

My mom and dad were the best parents in the world, but now that I have kids of my own, sometimes I feel a little funny about passing along the traditions of communication as they were passed along to me. I'm just not sure I have the tools to do what they did. In fact, I'm not even sure I want those tools.

For one thing, I can't make a good whistle. My dad had a strong, intimidating whistle. He'd whistle and other people's kids would run to my house. I've never understood what special techniques these super-whistlers employ. Coaches. Dads. Trains. They somehow place several fingers in their mouths (which sounds pretty unsanitary to me) and then commence to blow a high-pitched sound that can be heard from my street to space. I just don't have that. The only thing I get when I put my fingers in my mouth is a sinus infection.

Such a whistle commands respect among friends and foes alike. It is the whistle of generals and presidents. It screams that one does not have to scream. Yep, in terms of whistling, my dad was truly one of the greats.

My whistle? Not so high on the intimidation scale. "You kids get in here now!" Followed by the theme music from *The Andy Griffith Show*. "You think I'm joking? Right now!" Followed by the lovely sounds of a delicate bluebird's morning serenade outside your window. My kids have no idea I'm even calling them, but dogs and taxicabs line up ten deep in front of my house. Thanks, Dad. Thanks a lot.

And when it comes to emulating my mom, I am not sure I want to start with her advice. Quite honestly, Mom's advice was quite sound, but it was often just too late to matter. I remember being a kid and hitting my head squarely on the corner of the table—*boom!* From the other room, my mother's voice would ring out, "Careful!"

I'm sure glad you were here, Mom. Who knows what might have happened, Nostramomus.

She was always a big help when I would lose stuff too. "Hey, Mom, I can't find my wallet."

"Well, it's got to be somewhere."

That's smart thinking. I thought I was going crazy for a minute. You know, sometimes I like to look for things that don't exist. Thank you.

But her stellar wisdom continued. "Where'd you leave it last?" Oh, you're good. Thanks, Captain Obvious. I was on a totally different track. I was looking where I left it *first*.

I love my mom so much, but sometimes she could be the worst nurse in the world too. She believed in one cure-all method for all ailments both internal and external. "Mom, I don't feel too good."

"You need to go sit on the pot."

"But Mom, I think I—"

She would cut me off every time. "Pot! You need to sit on the pot! Yes, it's ancient wisdom that only I can conceive. Go sit on the pot. You'll feel fantastic, I'm telling you."

"But Mom, I think I broke my leg."

"Go sit on the pot."

I can see her at my funeral someday. "I told him to go sit on the pot. And now look!"

And I wish someone would have told my mom that Vicks VapoRub does not, in fact, cure everything. Those nights when I would go to bed and Mom would rub Vicks VapoRub all over my chest? Those were the longest nights of my life—in and out of consciousness as swirling fairy pizza delivery submarines chiseled plastic nightingales on my ceiling fan blades—turning my slightly stuffy nose experience into Woodstock. You know, Vicks—a gentle mixture of Vaseline and gasoline.

But nothing beats the superfluous directions my parents dole out. We'll be leaving their house to drive home when my mom waves from the porch and yells, "Okay, if y'all get tired, you can stay at a hotel. And if you're hungry, get something to eat, okay?"

Slow down there, Mom. Let me get a pen and paper because these are some real nuggets of wisdom you're throwing out there. You're like a Jedi master. Hey Yoda, what happens if we get thirsty? What happens then?

"Drink water, you will. Water. Hmm?"

And I doubt any human being with parents is immune to the most customary farewell so often shouted while the children are driving away. "Drive careful!"

Just once, I want my mom to actually verbalize the opposite just to see why it is so unnecessary to say it in the first place. "Drive fast and take chances. Cut people off, Sweet Pea! Use your road rage if you have to. Don't let people merge. Show 'em your tall finger!"

Tweet Thought @timhawkinscomic
When somebody asks me to do something I say "no worries," which means I'm not going to worry about not doing it.

Tweet Thought @timhawkinscomic
When giving someone bad news, you should surround it with two positives. Like "You're awesome. I'm suing you. You smell like fruit."

14

CHALLENGE FLAG

Marriage is a lot like a football season. Before it starts, everyone believes in the team and is expecting a perfect season. Sure, there are no wins yet to brag about, but more importantly, there are no losses to lament. Hey, even Browns fans like the Browns before the first game.

I think God designed the early feelings felt between young men and women to have this kind of preseason optimism. It is beautiful, really. I love it when I see young couples either on the verge of marriage or just recently married. Those kids know everything about marriage and they aren't afraid to brag about it too. "Our marriage is so amazing! It's just so spiritual. It's like we're joined . . . at the soul. And we finish each other's sentences all the time."

Married veterans hear this and laugh to themselves. I have been married for more than twenty years and I can truthfully say that we still finish each other's sentences. Just the other day I was like, "Hey, honey—"

"Make your own sandwich!" Wow, that was weird. I was just about to see if you wanted me to make you a sandwich, so yeah, we are definitely on the same page, sweetie. Soul mates. And just for conversation's sake, I know it's only a butter knife, but can you please put it down?

As I said, marriage is a lot like football. There are a lot of wins and a lot of losses—and the occasional concussion. One of the things I love about the NFL is the challenge flag. Wouldn't that be an awesome thing to have in marriage? An argument goes awry, so you throw the red flag and—*poof.* A referee suddenly appears out of your pantry. Nope, that's not weird at all.

The referee examines the situation and spends some time conferring with the two sides in private. He then retreats to a corner of the kitchen where a huge draped apparatus is set up. The replay booth. He sticks his head in the booth and spends what seems like an eternity watching and rewatching what just went down.

Eventually, he comes out of the booth and faces the couple. He fumbles to turn on his microphone that squeals for a second with feedback. "After further review, we have a personal foul on the male. He was not listening to the female's story at all. And there was an eye roll involved." The ref makes hand gestures as he emphasizes the crucial parts of each call.

The invisible women in the invisible stands erupt into wild applause while a collective boo arises from the men like the palpable stench of . . . well, men. "Get some glasses, ref! You're missing a great game! Hey Hank, what's that smell?" The kitchen and the proverbial grandstands of marriage have turned into utter bedlam.

But the referee is not finished with the call. "After even further review, we also have unsportsmanlike conduct on the female. She's told the same story four times this week." The ref's gesture for this call looks a lot like a traditional "talk to the hand." The women in the stands lose it. Nevertheless, the referee continues amidst the estrogen-induced jeering. "These penalties offset. Repeat conversation."

He blows his whistle, rewinds the play clock with a wide, overstated rotation of his arm, and motions for play to resume. You know, the game—marriage.

That's why I always tell newlyweds to establish a few ground rules in the beginning that could save each of you a world of hurt. Because I am a man, I can only speak from the male perspective on this one. But first of all, I think it's good for a husband to know that he is an idiot. Now I don't mean that he is actually stupid—because marriage is dissimilar from the actual world in every conceivable way. It is an alternate universe and in this other Stargate planet of matrimony, you are one or two brain cells smarter than an orangutan—and I'm not a Darwinist. I'm just telling you how God made us, and the earlier in your marriage that you accept this, the better.

So be proud that your idiocy only extends to your marriage. Unless, of course, you are an idiot out in the real world too. In that case, I can't help you. Just try staying away from sharp objects and avoid Facebook like the plague. That would do the trick for so many idiots out there. But for most of you, because of your marriage stupidity, do not assume your marriage will be as easy as just giving your wife flowers and then assuming she's good for three months. It doesn't work that way.

Marriage is like the stock market. It is constantly changing—usually for complex global reasons beyond the mental capacity of the average man to grasp—and you should constantly be checking it every day. You won't know why things happen, but you should at least recognize that they are happening. "Uh oh, that looks like a dip. She seems perturbed. I wonder what caused that? Ugh, must've been when I left that sock in the fridge. That's probably what happened there. Makes sense."

You can reason all you want, but just remember, the marriage market is subject to drastic changes, so buy and sell your comments very conservatively. "I love the way you changed your hair, darling."

"You do? So you didn't like the way it has been the last six years?"

Sell! Sell! Just try to make it to the closing bell before everything crashes. This thing—and I do not mean your wife—is bigger than you. It's bigger than me. It's bigger than all of us. So watch the subtle changes to avoid recessions that could lead to crashes. This is no game—this is your life.

And my final piece of advice comes straight from the Bible. "Never go to bed angry. Stay up. And plot your revenge. She's finally asleep; you can just think." That's in *The Message* Bible.

Tweet Thought @timhawkinscomic

Used my wife's facial scrub and it really opens up the pores. My face feels like an air hockey table.

Tweet Thought @timhawkinscomic

My wife says I have problems losing weight because I lack good bacteria. I think it's because I eat whole cakes before bed.

KRISPY KREMES

Today I turned forty. Yeah, I know, it's hard to believe that a guy this hot could be a whole two score years old. More like too sore. Or too sore to score. I'm still working it out—which is more than I can say for this sack of dirt I call a body.

My body is revolting—and I mean both the verb and the adjective. I don't think John Mayer was talking about this when he wrote "Your Body Is a Wonderland." He obviously was not forty yet. But man, that song would have been so different. What rhymes with varicose anyway?

As a former college athlete, I cannot recount the number of health classes I have taken in my life. It suffices to say the number is significant. I have learned all about the inception of life. The respiratory and endocrine systems. The miracles of human reproduction. How to exercise and maintain good heart health. Even how to keep one's colon clean.

Yet in all of my extensive studies, no one ever warned me about this. I need to go back and look for my old health textbooks and take a closer look. My guess is that there is a section in the back near the appendix simply called "Forty." It is probably not a large chapter. In fact, the imaginary section only has three pages with a few sentences printed in huge fonts across the tops of each—a living illustration of the sudden need for reading glasses when one's eyes age past forty years.

The first page simply says "Stuff you can't eat." Below it is a high-definition image of a Krispy Kreme donut. That's right. I'm no longer supposed to eat what I consider to be absolute divinity (not to be confused with the candy called divinity, which ironically tastes a lot like powdered sewage or a sponge covered in baby powder). No more Krispy Kremes? I'm not sure I want to live much longer if this is the quality of life. I doth protest.

Look, I don't really care if they can't spell "crispy" or "cream" correctly, those krazily konfused alliterators are doing some wonderful work over there. Eating a Krispy Kreme donut is like eating a baby angel. I don't even know what that means, but I doubt anyone out there would dispute me. Though it feels so wrong, it tastes so right. "Get in there, you little cherub. Let the momma-slappin' begin."

This just in: I heard that scientists are working around the clock in a groundbreaking attempt to engineer a sugar-free Krispy Kreme donut. What's the point? We have that already. It's called a bagel. Leave it alone, Donut Man. Critical mass is complete and the collective mushroom cloud of obesity continues to gloriously rise over our fine nation.

We have a Krispy Kreme store in my hometown. For a home-school family, this provides endless opportunities for culinary field trips. Sometimes I even remember to take the kids with me. A trip to the old Double K means I can press my face against the glass and watch them make the enchanted circles of life—each one waving to me as it goes by on that belt. God is so good. In fact, my dream is to go into Krispy Kreme and lie on that conveyor belt when it goes under the icing part . . . just get a full body glaze. Now that would make my body a wonderland.

I even wrote a song about Krispy Kreme to the tune of the old worship song that went "Holiness, holiness is what I long for. Holiness is what I need . . ." If you don't know it, try Google—this is the twenty-first century, you know. I'm not real sure why I have to keep helping you with stuff like this. And yes, the words *Krispy Kreme* should replace the word *Holiness*. Judge me if you want—I am unashamed. Well, that is not true, but since when did shame stop us from eating? That's what makes America great. Actually, that's what makes America jumbo. At any rate, the song went something like this:

KRISPY KREME

> Krispy Kremes, Krispy Kremes are what I long for
> Krispy Kremes are what I need
> Krispy Kremes, Krispy Kremes are what I want to eat
>
> Take some dough and form it
> Add some glaze and warm it
> Chew it up . . . transform it
> Oh Lord, Oh Lord
> Give me more!

When you turn forty, everything you hear about eating suddenly revolves around the theme of being healthy, even when it comes to cereal. But I say no, don't do it. Don't put these foreign substances in your body. Healthy cereal is wheat, barley, oats—it's mulch in a bowl. It's like I'm waking up every morning to the bottom of a hamster cage. I got a splinter the other day from my natural cereal—my bowl of Compost Toasties.

When I want a bowl of cereal, I want the real deal. Cereal is supposed to be fun, fruity, and magical. With marshmallows and a toy at the bottom. Yes, at the bottom. So you can plunge your germ-infested boy hand all the way down to retrieve it. When you open that box, unicorns should be jumping out. With horns and lasers. That's what cereal was meant to be.

Just below the donut is the image of something else . . . something none of us ever want to see on a food prohibition list. It is the picture of a pig. Ah, the majestic pig. So gallant. So powerful. So delicious. Who would think from looking at a pig that such gold lies just beneath that grotesque layer of dirty pink skin? But no more bacon for the forty-year-old. This is when you look at the page and notice watermarked tear stains. After all, this textbook is used.

I love bacon. I'd brush my teeth with bacon. I'm just kidding. That would be silly. I'd just floss with it. So when my wife said to me, "You can't have regular bacon anymore. I'll find you some bacon you can eat," my heart replied with a hearty, "Yippy skippy."

She went to the organic store and brought back this alien substance called turkey bacon. Turkey bacon is a failed bit from the get-go. This is not just true of the taste, but also of the appearance. Turkey bacon just stays flat when you cook it. Bacon is supposed to crinkle up when heated. It loves to pop in its own grease—serenading the eater with the alluring sounds of a fat-laden symphony of flavors. It actually sounds like applause, or even the crack of multiple gunfire in a Civil War skirmish. Turkey bacon? As flat as the earth before Columbus. It's like eating a meat-flavored Fruit Roll-Up. It's just not right.

Page two in the health book simply says, "Stuff You Can't Drink." Beneath it are a few more sentences than the first page, each detailing what liquids the forty-year-old male should now avoid. A good rule of thumb is that if it's normal in any sense of the word, then down the drain with it.

Now I'm supposed to drink diet soda instead of regular soda. In other words, brown carbonated water with a sweet tang to it that has you tasting metal for some reason. You know, diet soda. I remember the first diet soda: Tab. Tab stands for "Tasteless And Brown." In much the same way that the tab button on your computer keyboard advances your cursor to the next empty field on your screen, Tab soda advances your brain to the next empty reason to give up on life. It's like carbonated ipecac.

"Hey, you're really losing weight." Yeah, I'm dry heaving all the time.

Dairy's off the list too. Can't drink regular milk anymore. My doctor now has me drinking rice milk. You heard me right. Rice milk?

How are they producing this stuff? Those rice farmers must have tiny fingers and enormous patience to squeeze milk out of a rice nipple. "Y'all come back November, we'll have you half a cup, okay?" They say the wild rice have been known to kick you right in the face if you're not paying attention. They crave the open range of their ancestors.

Page three is quite possibly the most disturbing of the trio. The title says "Things You Cannot Get Rid Of." Then just below it is something you'd never expect: a picture of a Sasquatch covered in matted hair. Oh, too gross to bear? That's what I say—and that's *my* body.

My body's changing in ways they don't tell you about. As if the first set was not sufficient, I've got these new eyebrows growing in. Feels like fiber-optic cable or something growing out of my head. "Honey, have you seen the wire cutters? I've got guitar string growing out of my head."

Those strings apparently travel through my head into my ear canals. I've got ZZ Top in my ear hole now. Thanks, Lord. When I look at other older guys who can't seem to hear very well, I stop and tell them, "You don't need a hearing aid. You need a Weedwacker. You'll be hearing in Dolby in no time."

It's such a strange phenomenon. I'm losing all my hair up top, but the rest of my body looks like it is hosting an extended family of auctioneers down at the Alabama mullet convention. It's like a monk that quickly turns into Chewbacca as you move down. But the worst is that these same hairs are popping up in crop circle formations all over my back. If this is the aliens' best way to communicate, I'd say we have very little to worry about.

My kids are like, "Daddy, put on a shirt. That's disgusting!"

My wife doesn't help much: "What's wrong with you?"

I don't know. I'm turning into a hobbit. Why don't you go get me a comb, my precious? Let's cross the great canyon to Mordor! Urrgh! Actually, I hear they have a new Krispy Kreme over there in Mordor. We could probably lash together a hanging bridge out of all this back hair of mine.

If health class taught me anything, it's resourcefulness. So I shut the book to go lie down in the corner in a fetal position. I'm forty. This is my life now.

Tweet Thought @timhawkinscomic
My smoker friend says donuts are as bad as cigarettes, but I've never received a complaint about secondhand glaze.

Tweet Thought @timhawkinscomic
Found a four-leaf clover. Actually it was a Lucky Charms marshmallow stuck in my beard, but that still counts.

16

SHOES IN TWOS

Parenting is an incredibly rewarding experience. It is a journey through the portal of life leading one to find gentle streams of fulfillment flowing through rolling hills of adventure. It is a picturesque scene. That is, until it is overrun by wild animals . . . rising up in packs to conquer those rolling hills and soil those gentle streams. Setting up their own barbaric systems of governments and whatnot.

Those wild animals? Our children.

One cannot overstate what is spent in this art of war—I mean, parenting. And I wish money was all I was referring to. Yes, children can indeed eject dollars from one's wallet faster than romance from the parental bedroom. But money can be replaced. For that matter, romance can be restored. Just put a lock on the door and brush your teeth every now and again. But what those wonderful little loin fruits rob from us that can never again be replenished is a priceless commodity: time.

If parental time were generally spent on things that actually matter, perhaps I could stomach the whole issue a little easier. But no, the time I eternally donate to my children rarely concerns anything consequential. Answering endless questions about why Dad is so awesome? Negative. Taking them to monasteries to take vows of silence? If only. Teaching them the math skills they need to be successful in life? Impossible.

The truth is, all I ever do with the time spent in my house is look for my kids' shoes. That's it. The temporal substance of my parental core is completely defined by looking for shoes. You see, their shoes are never together. Do they come off their feet in the same location? Probably. It is most unlikely that their footwear fly off their feet at different random intervals as they run through the house, although not impossible. It is more likely that they actually take them off at the same time, leaving the pair together in one place.

But then something—the universe or a leprechaun or a wrinkle in time—intervenes to set in motion a daily impossibility. The right and left shoes levitate and are teleported to separate ends of the galaxy, a fact never revealed until the entire family is in a mad dash to leave the house in order to make it somewhere on time—and that one little child stands there holding his one shoe.

The tears begin to flow. The kid is usually pretty upset too. That's when the whole universe grabs its popcorn to watch the fireworks as Dad goes rampaging through the house looking for the lost shoe.

I'm sick of it, you Shoe Illuminati or whomever you are. From here on out, I refuse to play the top line of "Heart and 'Sole'" just because you play the bottom keys. I may be a mental primate, but this monkey ain't dancing no more.

So today, I instituted a new philosophy of taking back my time and sanity from the Shoe Mockers (not to be confused with our neighbors, the Shumakers, who are actually a delightful family). It was time to leave the house and the daily shoe rapture had caught them up and away. The traditional complaints began. "Daddy, I can't find my other shoe."

I breathed in deeply. "Get in the car. I don't care what's on your feet. Put a Ziploc storage bag on it; I don't give a rip." The little creatures can be so cute when you spook them. One of them opened its mouth to answer me, but I didn't give it the satisfaction. "No. I don't care if the shoes don't match. I don't care if you're wearing a rain boot and a flip-flop. I don't care!"

You see, though generally contrary to everything good and right in the universe, I think Walmart has it right in this one area: selling their shoes with that little plastic string to keep them together. Maybe we're not supposed to cut that. And think about it: the little ones would be easier to chase down too. Everybody wins.

Or perhaps we should just devalue the shoe enough that missing one is not that big of a deal. I think Payless has made an entire industry out of this concept. I mean, seriously. How do they make money at all? Buy one pair, get ten pairs free. They are like the ramen noodles of shoes.

I think Payless shoes are made out of ramen noodles. I sincerely do believe that. Next time I lose one, I'm just going to boil the other one and eat it. Maybe I could write their slogan for them—an adage I personally adopt when it comes to shoes, and occasionally hygiene: At Payless, We Care Less.

I think parents everywhere could really learn from this principle.

Tweet Thought @timhawkinscomic
You know stories about identical twins that are separated at birth then reunite later? That never happens with socks.

Tweet Thought @timhawkinscomic
Can't stand it when my kids ignore my phone calls. So I gotta walk into their room and wake them up for school.

17

DENOMINATIONS

Last night, I did two back-to-back sold-out shows for over five thousand people. This is crazy. Sometimes it's hard to believe that only a few years ago, I was driving a delivery truck for a grocery store. Before that, I was waiting tables at a restaurant in town. I would slip down to the local comedy club on my lunch breaks and try out new jokes, only to hurry back to finish my shift before my manager knew I was gone.

I was actually asked to share some of my experiences at a Career Day for a private school in Texas. Some of the jobs—real jobs, mind you—that were on my list included, but were not limited to: cat-sitter, apartment complex maintenance man, waiter at Chili's, youth pastor for a church without a youth department, intern for KZPS radio, paperboy, and substitute teacher.

Some of my experiences include answering a phone for GE Capital Mortgage, but I got fired when I quit answering the phones. I sold touchscreen kiosks to hotels and businesses. I rented cars for Enterprise. I planned events for salespeople through Cardinal Tracking—until I was laid off. I was then rehired at Cardinal Tracking until I tried nine months of comedy living out of my van. I hated the business side of comedy, so I came home and delivered groceries, driving a peach truck for an Internet grocer until the business folded. I then worked computer desk support for twelve hours a day for McLane Food Distribution until God finally brought it all together.

Now I do comedy.

My life consists of traveling around the country sharing jokes with people everywhere. It is an incredible existence and I am humbled beyond measure to live this life. By far, my favorite part of the lifestyle is meeting all different kinds of people. When I travel, I mostly perform in churches. Needless to say, there are many different kinds of churches and denominations out there that I have the honor of visiting. I have come to a place of personal sensitivity to the fact that each church has its own worship style.

Some people are more expressive in worship and some people are more subdued and subtle—but it's all good. That's what makes the family of faith so cool. There is room for people of all shapes, sizes, and personalities. I am beginning to think that I am divinely called to point out these differences—and then make fun of them. Yeah, people love that.

I suppose my observations of various denominations began at my shows. I have found that various congregants often congregate together like little hives, which often makes people of other congregational persuasions break out in hives. We could avoid these realities, as many do, and act like none of it is happening. Or we can laugh at—I mean, with—each other.

When I ask people at my shows what denomination they are, I find it odd how quickly and proudly they respond—well, most of them. I usually begin by asking who is Baptist, which produces an array of hands and some awkward cheers. I think even they themselves know that the Southern Baptist Convention is not that kind of convention— you know, the kind where you cheer. Or meet interesting new people. Or maintain a life force.

Some of them, for whatever reason, even lie about being Baptist. The nerve of some people. I can't figure this one out at all. The most obvious irony of lying about being Baptist is that one would forfeit their access to heaven over a religious matter. Does it really matter that much? Would you deny sprinkles and forfeit the whole donut? I think not.

How can I tell they are lying? Am I a prophet? Do I possess divine discernment? Negative, I just know that people on the front row who raise their hands claiming to be Baptists simply cannot be so. Baptists never sit on the front row. And if there's one thing that turns my stomach more than gross stereotypes, it's Baptists lying about the front row. For shame.

My favorites are people who refuse to accept a label at all. They call themselves "nondenominational" or "nondenom" for short. Some even go by just the term "non." In the spirit of the evolution of their name, I would continue to remove one more letter and simply say, "No." You are having an identity crisis for no reason. Just pick one already.

"Naw, we like all denominations. We're everything. We're Episcomethodyterianlic!" Just call yourself what you are: a Baptist church with a cool website. That's the nondenominational directive: be just a little cooler than the Baptists. Yeah, like a ten-minute trip to the Kmart clothing aisle wouldn't take care of that in a jiffy. Nondenominational folks are just Baptists who shop at the Buckle. Talk about the Bible Belt.

The "nons" also usually have a very cool coffee shop in their churches with a biblically catchy name like Holy Grounds. Jehovah Java. He-Brews. Are you hungry too? How about an exquisite pastry from the Daily Bread Café? You should order it unleavened style—they drizzle it with honey and throw it on the ground in front of you. I tell you what, that stuff is like manna from heaven! Heck, you can even order the bamanna nut muffin.

Some of the "non" churches have really grown. I attended one of these megachurches the other day and the parking lot was so big that its various sections had to be labeled like it was Disney World or something—except they named them after the fruits of the Spirit. So we parked our car in Goodness and then caught the nearest "Jesus Tram" to Worship Arena C7.

After church, I was riding the horizontal escalator down the Elijah Corridor—let me tell you, you can really get caught up in riding those things. I stopped by one of the Tithe Free gift shops to pick up a magazine to read on the tram ride back to my car. That's when I saw this couple with small children discussing where they parked. I was delightfully shocked by the hypocrisy of the whole event. Yep, I'm that kind of sicko.

Mom: "Where did you park the car, Harold?"

Dad: "I think I parked in Peace, dear."

Mom: "*Peace?* Urghh! I thought I told you to park in Self-control!"

Little Girl: "Daddy, I think we parked in Gentleness."

Dad: "Don't interrupt me!"

Somebody needs to order a decaf at He-Brews next time.

I love it when Catholics come to my shows because for whatever reason, those folks love to laugh. It's awesome. Now they don't usually clap too much, because they have a drink in their hand. The Catholics actually love that joke. Oddly enough, the only people who balk at it are the Baptists because I dared to acknowledge the existence of liquor in the universe.

"Liquor! Liquor alert! He said the L-word. Shield your eyes, kids! How much did we pay for this book again? Fetch me some wood for the fire . . . I've got a whole two hundred pages of kindling right here." Ironically enough, actual liquor would help this book burn up faster than you could say Moonshine Methodist. Oh, you quirky Baptists and your book burnings. Besides, you're the one reading my private journal, weirdo.

But all jokes aside, I tell people at my shows, especially young people, that they do not need drugs or alcohol to have a good time. It's better just to make the decision now that you don't need that stuff. Because there will always be that one person trying to pressure you into it all the time. It's something I can relate to.

I can just hear that voice now—all surfer-dude like Keanu Reeves. "Man, seriously, you are funny, seriously, but you'd be sooooooeeewwww funny hammered, bro! Dude, seriously, I'd love to see you wasted. Duuuudde, that would be sooooooeeeww funny, mahhhhn! Seriously."

And I'm like, "Leave me alone, Mom." I mean, there's enough pressure already.

Sometimes Mennonites will come to my shows, or as I like to call their movement, Amish Light. Somewhere out there, someone posed the eternal question: "I want to be Amish, but I also want my Xbox. Do I have an option here?" Why yes—yes, you do.

And I can usually tell if there are Mormons there by looking at how many bikes are parked outside the venue before the show. "Come on, peddle like you've never peddled before or we're going to miss the show. So help me, Jedidiah! If you get your dress pants caught in your bike chain again, no new name tag for you at Christmas. Hurry, you guys. We still have to stop by a few houses on the way!"

About here is where I usually throw in a polygamy joke, too, but people just can't take it. I don't know why everyone out there is so uptight these days. Look, we have to stop taking everything so seriously. Again, we must learn to laugh with each other.

But even if that's too hard to do, then it's like I always say: if you can't laugh at yourself, laugh at the Mormons.

Tweet Thought @timhawkinscomic
If you're sitting in church right now, look at a stranger and mouth the words, "I know what you did."

Tweet Thought @timhawkinscomic
I just shifted in my seat. Or what I like to call a "Presbyterian twerk."

18

JIM'S CLOSET

With each passing year, I become more and more aware that marrying Heather was the best thing I have ever done. She is an incredible woman. She's a strong woman. She's a patient woman. Why are all these so evident? Because I am an idiot. What was she thinking? Too late now.

But she has finely tuned female methods to counter my idiocy, and to be honest, they are pretty brilliant. For instance, she takes me to stores that men are never supposed to enter. The funny thing is, you can usually tell which stores men are not supposed to go in simply from the name on the sign. Stores like Bed Bath & Beyond. They should consider renaming that store for men. They could call it Aaaahhhh!

The name says it all. It lets one know if a store is for women or not. There is a store pretty close to our house that is a prime example: Kay's Closet. That one is no doubt a women's store—case closed . . . or caboodle closed, I should say.

There would never be a store for men called Jim's Closet. I am never going into Jim's Closet—or coming out of Jim's Closet, for that matter. Jim's Hunting Lodge? Jim's Poker Room? Jim's Big Screen Football Theater with Philly Cheesesteak Dispensers and Dr. Pepper Fountains on Every Recliner? Long name for a store, but I guarantee you men would be lined fifty deep to get into that one.

I don't know. I kind of wonder sometimes if Heather is using some of this against me like a weapon when she is frustrated. The other day, I had really made her mad about something—can't remember what it was. At any rate, she took me to this little French restaurant that was set up like a cafeteria. Once again, the name said it all. La Madeleine.

Men don't do "la" anything. There is no "la" bowling alley. No "La" Bass Pro Shop where you go to purchase "la" fishing lures or "la" shotgun shells. There is a "la" at the end of Cabela's, but whatever. Nope. She took me to La Madeleine. I must have done something terribly wrong to merit such female punishment.

But something about the experience caused me to rethink my entire concept of women punishing men in this manner. I began to hypothesize that their motives were much more complex. Deeper. Darker. Yes, there was something else afoot—and the foot was perfectly pedicured.

These visits to ultra-feminine stores and restaurants are like reprogramming centers. Like the brainwashing room in the show *Lost* where people were drugged and chained to chairs as they were forced to watch psychedelic shapes and weird propaganda for weeks on end. La Madeleine got to me. It's hard to describe it accurately because I'm pretty sure I blacked out at some point.

I vaguely recall seeing myself outside of my body as I went through the cafeteria line to order. I was glancing through the glass case at all the choices, searching for something masculine. A burger. A bratwurst. A buffalo wing. Anything to hang my emotional ten-gallon hat on. There was nothing, so I attempted to pick the lesser of the estrogen evils.

"Yeah, give me the . . . um, chicken salad croissant and some lobster bisque." But each word began seemingly releasing an invisible mist that drained my manliness and replaced it with pure femininity. The mist reeked of potpourri and hand lotion. Not realizing what was happening to me, I put my finger up to the corner of my mouth and continued with my order. "And . . . can I get that in a cup?"

It got worse. Much worse. I put my hands backward on my hips with my elbows pointed out—like Forrest Gump's stance on the front porch after his famous "I know what love is" conversation with Jenny. My voice began an unexpected ascent upward. "Oh, I need to make a substitution. Can I get the fruit cup instead of the chips? Okay, and an apple Danish—shouldn't but I'm gonna." Then I broke out into uncontrollable giggling.

"Do you have raspberry tea? With Splenda? Bonus! You know, all this eating's giving me an appetite for something else. Let's go to the candle store." Then I pranced around like Mick Jagger doing spirit fingers, which surprisingly is not that different from Mick Jagger doing his normal moves.

By the time I got done ordering there, I turned into my wife. Her plan had worked and La Timbulina was ready to plan the next bridal shower and personally bake and dress the petit fours to serve after teatime.

But sometimes, I think she is trying to get back at me for something. This is not an indictment. I so completely deserve it. I'm kind of surprised she doesn't do it more. But she is a better person than me. Better, but very different.

She asks me questions that no man on the planet would be capable of answering. Women have that knack. I don't mean to stereotype, but in this case it is true. I will be riding in the car with Heather just listening to the radio and contemplating how much I love my family when she pipes up with, "Three weeks ago you gave me that funny look in the car. Why?"

What does any human in their right mind or otherwise do with a question like that? "I didn't know there was going to be a pop quiz, Sugar Bear."

"No, what were you thinking when you gave me that look three weeks ago? What were you thinking?" She is serious. And I am seriously in trouble.

"To be quite honest with you, I don't know what I'm thinking right now. Can I use a lifeline or phone a friend or something?"

Another time, we were in the line at Walmart in the tabloid

section when she asked me this question: "If I weighed fifteen hundred pounds, would you still love me?"

Abort! Abort! You're coming in too hot! All I could do was put my head in my hands and wait for detonation. "It's a simple question, Tim! And why is it taking you this long to think about it? If I weighed fifteen hundred pounds, would you still love me?"

My mother always said honesty is the best policy. I guess I panicked and made the mistake of believing her. "Um, I'd visit?"

Give me a break. Fifteen hundred pounds is huge. I don't know! Maybe I'd take her to SeaWorld and try to make some money. In what universe is this scenario plausible? Apparently the only thing more flawed than her questions is my brain. Can I plead the Saks Fifth Avenue? How about another trip to La Madeleine? I'm trying here—I'm just a man.

For all the men out there struggling to find their way in this feminine world, I have written a song about a hero—a modern-day Odysseus who braved the watery elements and lived to tell about it. You can sing along in your head to the tune of the country hit "Jesus, Take the Wheel."

Cletus, Take the Reel

I was fishing last Friday on a lake in Mississippi
    in the humid summer heat
On a boat with my best friend Cletus who
    was sleeping in the backseat
Well the bites were slow and we were running
    low on chips and Gatorade
It'd been a long hard day

Felt a tug on the line and I didn't pay attention
    it was spinning way too fast
Before I knew it I was staring at a ten-pound shiny bass

Jim's Closet

When I tried to pull the fish inside I pulled
   a muscle in my upper thigh
I was so scared I threw my rod up in the air

Cletus, take the reel, take it from my hand
Cause I can't do this on my own
I'm letting go and I need your help fast
And if you don't my fish is gone
Oh Cletus, take the reel

Oh I'm letting go and I need your help bad
And if you don't my fish is gone
On this boat I'm on
Cletus, take the reel

Tweet Thought @timhawkinscomic
   "Dad, what's the secret with women?"
   "Make no mistake, son."
   "Yes?"
   "That's it. Good talk, son."

Tweet Thought @timhawkinscomic
The other day I played frisbee golf. Or golf frisbee. Or
whatever you call flinging a 9 iron into the woods.

19

SLAP YA MAMA

Some would say that eating food is a key to survival. I tend to agree. I have never attempted to test the theory and I am not a doctor, but I do have the Internet, which means I'm just as smart as anyone. Google is me much intelligence for nicely stuff.

Thus I consider myself to be an expert nutritionalician. I even have a framed certificate on my wall to prove that this title is legit. It cost me a whole thousand dollars. If you ask me, it was worth every penny—and I say that not in the colloquial sense, but because I paid for it completely out of my penny jar. Ironically enough, all those rolls of pennies weighed so much that the shipping fee to mail them off cost me more than the actual certificate.

Now that was worth every penny—in the colloquial sense this time. Try to keep up.

My point, if you will let me get there, is that my newfound and much-deserved expertise makes me feel so inclined to ponder the state of our current nutritional situation in America. For example, what is going on with this restaurant Chipotle? Are we just giving up on the idea of human-sized portions? Trying to order a burrito is like, "Yeah, just take a laundry bag and fill it with meat—that's what I want. And I don't want a tortilla; I want a duvet cover."

It gets worse. I was recently traveling through Oklahoma doing some shows when my bus passed by a Taco Bell Express. You heard me right—Express. You freaks need a punch line for that one? Are we in too big of a hurry for regular Taco Bell? Fifteen seconds is too long to wait for tacos?

I suppose we want our acid reflux faster and with more esophageal efficiency. Somewhere in Japan, a kid just solved a calculus equation. Somewhere in Oklahoma, a kid just shortened his life span by three years when he inhaled seven tacos at once in an effort to lower his elevated blood pressure caused by his extreme anger over said tacos taking more than three minutes to be delivered to his gullet.

Seriously, how is Taco Bell going to get my food to me any faster than they already do? Are they going to shoot it out of a cannon as I drive by? "I'll take a number two—now! Come on. I want immediate diarrhea, chop-chop! Let's skip the middleman. I'm late for my nap."

Truthfully, though, I love eating in the South. Down south, they have some good restaurants, but they also have some questionable ones. A southern favorite seems to be Cracker Barrel. Let me tell you, they love their Cracker Barrel down there. Eating at the ole CB is an event worth bathing for. "Aw, we gonna take you to the Barrel, Timbo. Gonna get our heart palpitations on like Donkey Kong!"

But the thing is, the CB is not that great. It's not really the food I have a problem with; it's the atmosphere. Eating at Cracker Barrel is like eating at a garage sale. There's stuff hanging all over the walls— and rusty farm equipment dangling over your head.

"Excuse me, ma'am, but can we get a table that is not located directly under the horse castrator? And that is a thin thread holding up that Sword of Damocles." I just want to eat, not take my life into my own hands. And the requests to the servers become even weirder than that. "Sir, I need some more golf tees for this triangular game. Well, shucks. Six left? Guess I'm an 'ig-no-ray-moose.'"

And also, they don't have omelets at the Cracker Barrel, even though it is supposedly the quintessential southern destination for breakfast. "Ma'am, let me get this straight: y'all don't have omelets?"

The brown-aproned waitress kindly replies with the southern charm that makes me love traveling below the Mason-Dixon Line.

"You know, sweetie, we sure don't. I guess what you see is what you get, sugar."

"Hmm, okay. Well, let me ask you a few questions. Y'all got eggs?"

"Yeah, we got eggs."

"Y'all got some peppers, sausage, and mushrooms?"

"Yessir."

"Y'all got some cheese?"

"Yeah, we got cheese."

When my point is obviously not speaking for itself, I make a simple folding gesture to connect the dots. "You think you could think outside the box? I'm sure we can work something out, kitty. I'll draw you a schematic if I have to."

But I love those southern waitresses at the Cracker Barrel because they are just so nice and sincere. And as I discovered, they are also very descriptive—even to the point of confusion.

The other day, I was just trying to order food and I decided to ask a few questions to help with the decision. I was not at all ready for her answers.

"How are the biscuits and gravy?" Seems like a simple inquiry.

"Oh, honey, they'll make you wanna slap ya mama!" I was as confused by her tone as I was by her words because apparently, slapping one's mother in the South is considered to be a good thing. All this talk of southern hospitality and chivalry? Somewhere in southern history when these cultural mainstays developed, a key concept was excluded—and it's a big one. The striking of one's mother should have made the list as a negative, but instead, it is considered the pinnacle of one's ecstasy when eating.

I've heard that a belch is a compliment to an Italian mother after eating her meal. Or saying something is the "dog's bollocks" is a good thing in England. I guess complimenting a southern mother is an openhanded blow to the jowl. "Hey guys, I gotta go. Tell Momma thanks for the meal if and when she comes to."

I just sat there. Slowly, as not to spook her, I replied, "Then . . . I don't think I'm going to order the biscuits and gravy, being that my mama's here and all. That would be kind of awkward. How are the pancakes?"

"Oh they make you want to hit ya daddy with a baseball bat!"

It's just too much. Do you have a less violent menu I could look at? I don't want to hurt anybody. I just want some food.

I hear the apple crisp will make you wanna slap a belching dog's bollocks.

Tweet Thought @timhawkinscomic
On the next *Mythbusters*: Does slappin' ya mama make you wanna eat a delicious biscuit?

Tweet Thought @timhawkinscomic
New meal plan. Been eating smaller meals throughout the day. With large meals in between. And then more small meals.

I DON'T CARE
ANYMORE

My forties are not being very kind to me. I've asked them to, but the only responses I get come in the form of midnight leg cramps and apathy. I prefer the apathy. Honestly, it sounds worse than it is—you know, like a colonoscopy. Okay, bad example. That really is worse than I thought it would be. Thanks for the memories, forties . . . although even those are getting harder to hold on to. Wow. I should see a therapist. Nah, this journal will do nicely.

My apathy is not related to those things in life that actually matter. I'm not a monster. Well, I am growing hair on my back and most orifices at an X-Men rate of speed. I'm just two bottles of blue hair dye and a few PhDs in astrophysics away from becoming the stunt double for Dr. Hank McCoy—the Beast.

But again, my apathy is not directed toward anything in life that really matters. All I hold dear is still held dear. My faith. My wife. My children. My stash of sour cream and onion Pringles hidden in my sock drawer. Yep, all of my life's greatest priorities remain intact.

However, there are a lot of things I don't care about anymore. None. Zilch. Nunca. Like I don't care what people think of me. Let them stare. Let them find out what they will about me and draw whatever conclusions they desire—even if those conclusions are to call 911 or post an Instagram photo with the hashtag #rockbottom or #humanfails. I don't care. So what if the only thing longer than their ridiculous hashtags are my nose hairs. I'll braid that mess and tweet the carnage.

So what if people judge. Yes, I've used a Walmart baggy for a wallet. I don't care. I've clipped my toenails on airplanes. I don't care. I've used Febreeze on my armpits on a Sunday morning. I don't care. I drink straight from the milk jug when I'm at other people's houses. I don't give a rip. "Hey man, make yourself at home." Don't say it if you don't mean it. I will. I'll drink your milk. I'll rearrange your furniture. I'll spank your kids. I'll run on your treadmill while wearing your yoga pants, you hippie.

Why should I change now? What's the point? I'm going to relish my forties. I made it. Besides, I'm still the same guy. I'm no different now than I was in my twenties or thirties. Well, maybe only a few differences. I've gained a few pounds. My hair's a bit thinner. And my nipples point sideways. Like a horse's eyes. Again, minor differences.

I'm writing this in the privacy of my own journal because for whatever reason, Christians out there freak out when you acknowledge that you have nipples. Seriously? Where's the mystery here? Do they think that if we never mention them that they won't exist and embarrass us or something?

I don't care anymore. The truth is, I'm a Christian man with nipples and they're now pointing east to west. Whatever relationship these bad boys once enjoyed with one another has now descended into apathy—I guess they take after me. I'm like Papa Nipple. But they don't even care about each other anymore. The only time they meet anymore is when I lay on my back and they touch each other behind me. Now that's an unexpected nipple reunion spot right there. It's ridiculous.

So excuse me if I am a bit apathetic these days. Should I be blamed? Look at what is happening to me. And furthermore, I'm over stupid things related to my body—like the names we give certain body parts. I find it hilarious and wrong that they call it a belly button. There's no button there. The button is long since gone. Call it what it is: a gut hole. It's a big cavernous area and I don't want to look in there. What am I going to find? Look honey, there's an Oompa Loompa squatting in my gut hole. A Chilean miner? A couple of Duggar kids? Look honey, there's Jim Bob Duggar squatting in my gut hole.

And *squatting* is a confusing term to me. We use it to describe someone who takes up uninvited residence in an abandoned building or home. Can we not call it something else less visually descriptive— and consequently less indicative of someone using the bathroom? I know that's how the Chinese do it. There's just a hole in the ground and you squat and hope for the best. It's kind of like golf. So, over there if you miss the mark, you don't need a plunger—you need a putter.

But come on. People living in an abandoned warehouse do sit down like normal people. They sleep. How about "sitters" or "sleepers" —or "in-laws"? "Squatters" just sounds like they wouldn't be staying very long in one place—which is true, but just not for the same reasons the name denotes. I guess if someone's going to be squatting in my gut hole, I need clarification because the worst-case scenario is the weirdest and most disgusting thing I could ever imagine.

The whole previous squatters thought process is a case in point that the forties are a place of mental and physical digression. It's depressing. I can't even buy cool clothes anymore. I went into Dick's Sporting Goods to purchase one of those cool Under Armour workout shirts. I know that these things are so tightly fitting that they display every contour of your body, but it looked so good on the mannequin. Mistake.

I didn't even try it on; I just bought it and took it home. When I finally put it on, I stood in front of the mirror. It looked like I was smuggling a family of woodchucks. I immediately tried to take it off, but it had me in its evil clutches, adhering to my skin like stink to a middle schooler. With every attempt to take it off, its boa constrictor grip only tightened. I spun around in circles like a wild banshee trying to finagle it over my head, but it wasn't budging.

In the middle of this awkward waltz with midlife insanity, my daughter walked in the room to ask me a question. Upon beholding me in such a vulnerable state, she immediately began dry heaving. "Oh Daddy, what have you done? Not the Under Armour!"

She pulled out her iPhone and dialed a number. She must have put it on speaker phone because I heard the answer on the other end: "911, what's your emergency?"

"There's a woodchuck eating my father. Get over here quick!" Then she pointed to my neck and screamed, "Daddy, its tail!"

"That's my chest hair. Shut your mouth."

It was an awkward conversation with the firemen and paramedics, to say the least. They did bring out the Jaws of Life, though, and were able to extract me roll by roll from the Under Armour shirt. They should put a warning label for older men on those things. It could simply read: "Forty? Don't." I took it back to the store even though it was in two tiny pieces that fit into the palm of my hand. It had shrunk back to its original size like a deflated balloon. It wasn't the only thing that was deflated.

It's not fair. The forties bring with them so many paradoxes. I'm finally old enough to afford any kind of food I can dream of, yet I'm not supposed to eat it. Look, I'm the man of the house. I take care of business. I pay the bills. I am the man. So why do I have to hide in a corner of my laundry room to eat a stinking bowl of Lucky Charms?

My wife breaks through the door and forcefully demands an explanation from me. "Tim. Not again. How many times are we going to have to go over this? Why are you eating Lucky Charms?"

It's only because there is a full-size mirror on the wall that I catch a glimpse of what I truly look like in that moment. I'm hunched over in the floor guarding that tiny bowl like Gollum. My dampened hair is matted with milk and a few randomly embedded blue marshmallow moons and purple horseshoes. My eyes flash with lightning like an unbridled beast cornered in a cage—overtaken by the protective instincts of the wild.

"Because they're magically delicious! Don't you read the box?"

Then I proceed to wildly ferry as many bites as possible into my filthy gut trap—my mouth, that is, not to be confused with my gut hole (see previous madness)—before anyone can rip the sugary sweet treasure from my stickily gnarled fingers.

I guess that's what I get for squatting in the laundry room. Wait . . .

Tweet Thought @timhawkinscomic
The 3 things I want said at my funeral are: "He made the world better," "His family will miss him," and "Hey! He's awake!"

Tweet Thought @timhawkinscomic
Proverbs says, "Like a dog that returns to his vomit is a fool who repeats his folly." Which pretty much explains my relationship with Waffle House.

CHRISTIAN CUSS WORDS

There are not many things I regret, except that I sometimes have so little to regret. This sort of regret is almost exclusively reserved for Christian kids who grew up in church. Youth group culture is truly a microculture, complete with its own unique dialect, musical artists, and fashion trends. (I still own my old "To Hell with the Devil" T-shirt from my very first Stryper concert.)

For the Christian kid, any opportunity to drop a faux curse word was the greatest of all thrills. We had a plethora of phrases that incorporated all the four-letter words our "secular" friends were using so sinfully, but in completely different and creative ways. It was like an art form: Christian cussing. Witness intact.

I remember it like it was yesterday. We had to start small and build up slowly—these were dangerous waters and getting it wrong could cost one dearly. We would always start with the word *hell*, but in a purely geographical sense. Some people get confused about this and try to use it in other ways. Specifically, I always found it odd how people often use the phrase "fun as hell." Which part exactly are they referring to? Do they mean the "eternal torment" fun or the "lake of fire" fun? Just curious. Look, stick with geography—that's the secret.

The devil goes straight to hell.

Simple. True. Impervious to judgment. Theologically sound. Saying this would perk the ears of my mother, but upon further review, would keep me from any trouble whatsoever. But we would never stop there. Christian cussing was like a drug—not to be confused with actual drugs. We would never try those.

The next word a Christian kid could use was *damn*, but only used in the same sense as *hell*—geographical. And of course, the entire phrase had to always refer to the devil. That was just another one of the necessary components to successful Christian cussing. Talk about the devil and everything stays clean. Yes. The irony here is thick.

The devil is damned to hell.

Whew, that was close. By this point, any respectable youth "groupee" would be nursing a nervously holy sweat. Said sentence was now teetering like a highly stacked game of Jenga. Now the stakes were high and one bad move could land a clean Christian kid a dirty mouthful of soap.

But we just couldn't stop. The next addition had to be perfectly and delicately placed. It was a true biblical word and could only work if one had the grammatical creative chops to Christian cuss at this level.

The devil will ride on a jackass when he is damned to hell.

The trifecta complete, a masterpiece of brilliant aprofanity was born. Elegant. Sophisticated. Obviously logical—I mean, of course Lucifer would be riding a stubborn donkey on his journey to experience the flames of eternal damnation. Why would he not?

Of course, there was always the occasional overzealous youth pastor who would get a little too froggy with the Christian cussing. Amateurs. This was fire we were playing with and those who approached the flames haughtily were begging to get burned—or fired. See what I did there?

Usually, the target the young pastor was shooting for went something like this: "I don't want to scare you into heaven, but I do want to scare the hell out of you." Masterful? Nah. Solid? I suppose. It had theological soundness, but definitely lacked the subtle nuances used by the greats. But all in all, it would suffice to ruffle Sister Mildred's feathers, yet leave the young preacher with complete plausible deniability.

But unfortunately, on more than one occasion the whole attempt was botched and well-meaning young men were left searching for secular employment. Casualties of the dangerous craft of Christian cussing. "I don't want to scare you into heaven, but I will scare the hell out of that jackass devil . . . *wait*!"

Happy trails, Pastor Chad. You'll probably enjoy your new job at the Methodist church more anyway. Open hearts. Open minds. Open doors. Open containers.

I have actually spearheaded a movement to provide a list of appropriate Christian cuss words for the vast majority of the religious populace who are just not ready to try the real words and succeed. How many youth pastors have to lose their jobs before we change the system? Thus, I actually requested from my Facebook and Twitter followers that they submit their favorite words of this persuasion. And I received over ten thousand replies from you freaks.

So with a little help from my friends, I have compiled a list of the top 100 Christian cuss words that will suffice to help you express yourself, yet not develop too much of a testimony while doing so. The best method is to read this as fast as possible out loud in order to really gain a feel for flow and discover which ones work best for you.

Here they are in random order: shucks, rats, gadzooks, shizzle, toot, crapola, holy moly, holy stinking moly, holy guacamole, holy mackerel, holy cow, holy smokes, holey buckets, bucket head, turd, fiddlesticks, fiddle faddle, flippin, horse hockey, horse feathers, horse patootie, phooey, bull twinkies, shut the front door, criminy, criminitly, cripes, good gravy, good grief, great googley moogley, great Caesar's ghost, h-e double hockey sticks, bleep, son of a biscuit, son of a biscuit eater, son of a Baptist preacher, son of a bacon bit, son of a nutcracker, son of a motherless goat, for heaven's sake, for the love of Pete, for Pete's sake, for crying out loud, jumpin Jehoshaphat, raza fraza raza fraza, crud, crud muffin, gee willikers, mother of pearl, shucky darn, nerts, Fahrvergnügen, cotton pickin, heavens to Betsy, Mylanta, what the hey, snot, bull snot, booger snot, fartknocker, jeepers, geeze Louise, Mother Francis, Judas Priest, Bob Saget, Pat Sajak, sheesh, booty, shut your pie hole, kiss my grits, malarkey, doo doo, caca, Bolshevik, gosh, what the what, what the devil, wingnut, ticked off, jackwagon, heck, shoot, dang, darn, darnit, dad burnit, dag nabbit, con sarnit, confound it, doggonnit, dad blame it, dad gummit, dad blast it, and suck eggs.

Save the youth pastors. Help them learn the right words.

Does not the previous description prove the thickness of the fog my brain has been enveloped in for so many years? That is why I can say something so illogical as: "My biggest regret is having too few regrets." What I mean is that sometimes I wish I had a better testimony. It is a desire carried over from hearing so many "incredible" testimonies as a kid and thinking, *This guy's testimony is awesome. I hate my testimony. I wish I was addicted to heroin. But no. I had to grow up in a somewhat functional family situation. It's just not fair. Why can't I be a crack addict who robbed Fort Knox using nothing but a can of hair spray and a plastic ice cream scoop? Thanks a lot, God.*

Me? My testimonial moments involve less awesome things and more stupid things. They would not make a very good made-for-TV movie. They are bland. Embarrassing. Pathetic. If only I had more to regret.

For example, just a few nights ago, I was doing a show at a venue for about two thousand people. I did pretty well and after the show, they took me to this room that had a table and Sharpie on it. There was a line of people in the hallway waiting to get my autograph. Trust me, anytime this happens, it is a personal honor that I never take lightly. About a hundred people lined up to meet me and receive my John Hancock on their poster, CD, or T-shirt. I'm thinking, *Oh sweet! I feel pretty good about myself right now.* My own thoughts foreshadowed my impending doom.

The first lady in line walks up to the table and peppily says, "Would you put your favorite Bible verse under your name for me? Just your name and your favorite Bible verse."

"Um, sure . . . no problem." Well, my favorite Bible verse is Psalm 34:8, which says, "Taste and see that the LORD is good; happy are those who take refuge in him." But for whatever reason on that night, I blanked. I totally forgot the verse. I could remember that it was somewhere in the book of Psalms. But the line in the hallway was getting longer, so I figured I just needed to pick a verse and let it ride.

How bad could it be? The whole Bible—and especially the book of Psalms—should be a safe place to do guesswork. I mean, I could understand having trouble if I were to "eeny-meeny-miney-mo" from one of the first five books, ending up referencing one of those "Habishath begat Elibashath begat Phiboshath begat . . ." parts. Contrary to popular belief, sometimes there is no safety in Numbers. Is this thing on?

But this was Psalms, for the love of David! I picked Psalm 38:7 out of thin air. Like an idiot, I signed every piece of merchandise that night with this same verse. "Tim Hawkins—Psalm 38:7. Hope you enjoyed the show!" I was driving home that night and I suddenly felt the need to pray. It was a sinking feeling. "Oh Lord, I hope that was a good verse. Oh Lord, could you change the scripture if it's not? Just for one night?"

But yea I say, God did not hear my prayer. I got home and looked up Psalm 38:7. To my horror it said, "Lo, I have a painful disease in my loins . . ."

What are there, like a billion verses in the Bible? And I chose that one? And I signed it a hundred times. And then I sent it out in my own little mission field. "Go. Take the Word. Don't forget my little loin problem. Build schools and hospitals. Don't forget my loin disease . . ."

I'm certain that people looked it up and made a big deal about it. I can see that first lady in line gathering her family around the living room for a quiet time. "Come on, kids, let's sit down. Let's read this verse. Billy Earl, turn the television off and let's see what that blessed [pronounced "bless-ED"] Tim Hawkins had to share with us from

God's Holy Word. Here it is. Psalm 38:7. Shhh! It says, 'Lo, I have a painful disease . . .'"

She trails off into a silent, frightful place. Then she erupts into hysteria. "I shook his hand! I shook his hand! I shook that pervert's hand! What'll I do? Billy Earl, go get the hand sanitizer and some matches!"

Nope, never going to see my testimonial verse cross-stitched on a throw pillow.

Tweet Thought @timhawkinscomic
Is it "up the wazoo" or "out the wazoo"? I'm working on a Common Core math problem.

Tweet Thought @timhawkinscomic
A friend will stick closer than a brother, and a brother will hit you with a stick.

RECOMPUTING

Traveling so much for a living has afforded me quite the opportunity to marvel at the vast advancements in geography and technology across this great nation. It's amazing what all I get to see from sea to shining sea. *Si?*

New York. Seattle. Los Angeles. Atlanta. These sprawling urban areas are unto themselves monuments to the foresight of our architectural forefathers—and foremothers, too, I suppose. Never heard of a foremother, but I don't think they should be left out of the mix. Like I always say, we've got to end this women's suffrage right now. They've suffraged enough and no one seems to care about their plight. If I'm anything, I'm progressive. Who's with me?

At any rate, these massive skyscrapers and buildings stretching into the sky are modern-day marvels. I can't even imagine the amount of time spent dreaming and drawing so that such ornate masterpieces of twisted steel and tempered glass can ascend high into the city skyline. And then to have the wisdom to plan the infrastructure to get people and automobiles in and out of these areas? Brilliant. Thousands of miles of highways, streets, and intersections, each meticulously designed to work together in engineering harmony. These guys are geniuses.

And then there's Dallas.

I recently flew into Dallas and had to rent a car. Who built this city—munchkins from Oz? When Kevin Costner heard that mysterious cornfield voice say, "If you build it, they will come," someone in Dallas must have been stuck in a wind tunnel and heard it a bit differently: "Get the people to move here, then build the roads." And that is just what they did.

It's like someone decided to build a series of bridges—to nowhere. I was driving on one and it just stopped in midair. When they say "off-ramp," they aren't kidding. It was like an off-ramp in a *Dukes of Hazzard* episode. My car just froze in midair as the song "Good Ol' Boys" was suddenly interrupted by Waylon Jennings's southern commentary on the situation, "Oh poop."

Somewhere in a shadowy high-backed chair, a Dallas civil engineer was watching the whole event via a traffic camera while stroking the bleached white fur of his villainous feline. "Ha ha ha! He's off the ramp now!" Thanks a lot, Dr. Road Rage.

I theorize that a lot of the new technology we are seeing today is being developed in reaction to issues such as these. Bad road planning, meet your arch-nemesis: GPS. I love GPS because it tells you what to do. It's like idiot-proofing your travel adventure, without making you feel like an idiot. If wives would have taken this attitudinal approach in helping husbands navigate over the years, I doubt GPS would have ever been needed.

But alas, mankind has finally found a passenger who actually knows which way to go, yet also understands the subtle nuances of how to tell you minus the sting of sarcasm or ridicule. Now that is my kind of technology. No need to plan. No need to look ahead. No need to even keep your hands on the steering wheel—just let the rumble strip be your north star. Wait . . .

My point is that the GPS just allows me to drive. To feel the thrill of the open road. The wind in my hair. The sweet taste of diesel exhaust. And when it speaks, it does so in soothing tones of confident reassurance. "Turn left now."

Why thank you, GPS. And how are you today?

"Turn right up ahead."

A lovely idea. More tea and crumpets?

"Turn around and go the other way."

What? Have you been talking to my wife again, GPS?

But when I get into Dallas, even the GPS loses heart. "You're on your own. Your guess is as good as mine. Good luck and may the Force be with you, Luke." Should have sprung for the deluxe software edition. Or possibly a protractor.

The most refreshing part of using GPS happens at the exact moment I used to be most irritated: when I make a wrong turn. Look, it's going to happen. Why should we be made to feel like idiots just because we get lost sometimes—on the way to my mother-in-law's house?

But in terms of attitude and tone, GPS stays the course. Yes, that is intended. When you do something bad, it simply responds with, "Recomputing... Recomputing..." It does not say, "You moron!" or "You idiot!" or "My mother was right about you!" No, just "Recomputing..." I love that.

In fact, I want Life GPS. Just tell me what to do in my life. "Your fly is down." Thanks GPS. "Purchase gum. Your breath smells like a sewer." Indeed it does, GPS. What would I do without you?

They could even design different versions of Life GPS for various people groups—like Redneck GPS. Rednecks need GPS pretty badly. I should know because sometimes I are one. Once I was in a small southern town and I had no idea how to get anywhere, so I stopped to ask an old guy for directions. "Hey partner. How do I get to the mall?"

He temporarily paused his whittling and slowly leaned forward in his rocking chair. His bones creaked with the sounds of a rich life history and I knew that deep wells of wisdom were priming to spring forth from the fathoms of his being. After a long, drawn-out breath that seemed painful for the both of us, he finally replied, "From here?"

No, from Pakistan. I was thinking about starting from there. Can you just draw me a map, slappy? Yep, Redneck GPS would help in so many ways, although the digitized voice would have to be adjusted quite a bit to speak the regional vernacular. "Turn left at the Wawlgreens. Ya gonna see a pit bull and a go-cart, but jus' keep a-goin'. Nope, ya went too far. Re . . . Recomp . . . Uh, we're doin' it again."

Another helpful version would be Marriage GPS. Now that is what we men really need. Just tell us what to do because guys actually don't have a clue what is happening.

GPS: "Say something about her hair." Ooh, good thinking, GPS.

Me: "Hey, what's up with your hair?"

GPS: "Recomputing . . ."

Tweet Thought @timhawkinscomic

I wish I knew:

1. how electricity works
2. if Bigfoot is real
3. why Carrie Underwood's teeth are all the same size

Tweet Thought @timhawkinscomic

Coins in my car's cup holders are stuck in some type of mystery syrup.

YOU CAN'T HANDLE
THE TRUTH

There is no doubt in my mind that marriage is a precious gift from God, but my wonderful wife still confuses me sometimes. Well, most times. I don't blame her, though. I'm confused about a lot of things. I'm just an animal. People talk about the "fight or flight" response. What about the "head tilting confusion" as a response? I'm the husband; I'm supposed to be confused.

Yet I cannot figure out if my wife thinks I'm a genius or an idiot. I say this because she constantly asks questions of me that indicate either she is very secure and wants to watch me dance like a puppet, or she is completely broken and truly thinks I hold the answers to mend her back together. Either way, I'm not sure what to do.

For example, she consistently asks me a certain question late at night. From what my friends tell me, their wives do the same thing. The doors are locked and the kids are finally asleep. The lights have been turned off and even the dog is settling in for some quality sleep. I lie down on my side of the bed, which is only like six inches after my wife stretches out and claims her own territory. So there I lie, one leg hanging off the bed and the blanket barely covering my outside shoulder, ready to slip into blissful and oft denied unconsciousness.

Suddenly, Heather sits straight up in bed and death grips my arm, digging into my flesh with her fingernails. "What was that sound?" Sound? Do you mean the sound of sweet silence I was lost in? The sound of a good night's sleep that was trying to grace me with its rare presence? The sound of your own neuroses disturbing me yet again? Because honestly, those are the only sounds I hear.

Of course, I say none of this, choosing instead a safer response that will not lead to my own demise. "What sound, honey? I didn't hear anything."

"No, I heard it. It sounded like someone's downstairs—you need to go see what it is."

Once again, confusion. I know she has seen me with my shirt off a few times. Either she is delusional and believes me to be much stronger and more capable of winning a violent encounter with a criminal who has broken into my home than I actually am, or she hired the criminal and is trying to take me out. Of course, I can't vocalize what's in my mind at that moment because it would be inappropriate, and not to mention, humiliating.

But oh if I could. "You get up and look. News flash: I'm just as scared as you are. I'd rather die wearing a duvet than out there freezing."

Instead, I usually choose the right answer. "Okay, I'll go look." I keep my shirt off, just in case—not to intimidate the assailant, but perhaps to incite his laughter for a split second while I reach for an umbrella or an orange peeler or anything else I can find to use as a makeshift weapon.

I imagine a biblical David and Goliath–style conversation would ensue between us. I envision him wearing a black leather vest with bare arms exposed, chiseled with muscles and inked up with graphic green images of him strangling little punks like myself. His tattoo artist is quite the talent. I wonder if he'd do a little orange butterfly on my hip?

At any rate, I picture him holding a baseball bat and standing nine feet tall. His voice rings out in a low growl, "Am I a dog that you send this small, shirtless girly man out against me with kitchen utensils and high cholesterol?" The rest of the story is probably best left unwritten, but it suffices to say that it does not end well for the dog—well, more like the poodle man.

But the questions about a noise downstairs are not the only ones that are lose-lose for the husband. In fact, I wish there was some sort of cue that would give men a heads-up that they are in trouble. Perhaps a whistle? A duck call? A muted trumpet playing "wa wa wa" in descending notes? Maybe even just a good old-fashioned game-show buzzer. *Aannnnck.*

The right answer is not the only variable at play here. Timing of one's response can be equally as crucial to marital survival as content. There can be no hesitation. No split-second moment for an eye twitch or foot shuffle. It must be seamless. "Do these pants make my butt look fat?"

"Umm . . ."

Aannnnck. Sorry grasshopper, but you had to think for a nano-second. Despair awaits you, my friend. Game over. "Tell him what he wins, Bob." Well, Tim, you win an all-expense paid vacation to seven nights on the sleeper sofa, courtesy of your own stupidity. And that's not all! You will also enjoy a week's supply of crow to eat, coupled with a steady round of Guilt Complex B12 injections to compensate for your obvious disdain of your wife's appearance. You're a monster.

Marital conversations are tough in real life. But around our house, they are even beginning to be tough in non-real life as well. I blame the advent of Netflix. Ever since Heather and I signed up for Netflix, we have thoroughly enjoyed watching movie after movie with the touch of a button. It's awesome.

But I fear that all this movie watching is beginning to bleed over into our communication—a quadrant of our life already susceptible to unexpected catastrophe. That is to say, it is susceptible to the fact that I am a man and she is a normal human. These movies may be starting to influence our arguments.

My wife walked in the other day and said, "Hey, um, did you leave your underwear on the bathroom floor?" It was a simple question that in years past would have solicited a simple answer from a simple person. But for some reason, I was feeling more complicated, to say the least. "Are those your underwear on the bathroom floor?" she repeated.

"Uh, well let's see! Are those my underwear on the bathroom floor? I hope so! Because if they aren't, that's a whole other conversation."

Remember, though—Heather had been watching Netflix with me. I was not the only one under its deceptive trance.

She fired back with, "I want to know!"

"What do you want from me?" I retorted.

"I want the truth!"

"You can't handle the truth! Honey, we live in a world where men leave their underwear on the bathroom floor. Who's going to pick them up? You? The kids? I have a greater responsibility than you can possibly fathom. You weep over my Hanes. You curse my Fruit of the Looms. You have that luxury. You have the luxury of not knowing what I know. That my laziness, while tragic, probably saves lives. And my underwear, while grotesque and incomprehensible to you, saves lives. You don't want the truth because deep down in places you don't talk about at parties, you want them on that floor. You need them on that floor. We men use words like *boxers*, *briefs*, *whitey-tighties*. You use them as a punch line. I wish you'd just say 'thank you' and be on your way. Otherwise, pick up your own underwear and stand at post. Either way, I really don't care what you think you are entitled to!"

She looked at me blankly and then kindly said, "Well, pick them up."

"Okay," I replied.

It may be time to read a book or two.

Tweet Thought @timhawkinscomic

Husband, the next time your wife overcooks something, don't wince and say it's "burnt." Marvel and say it's "caramelized."

Tweet Thought @timhawkinscomic

What you don't know won't hurt you unless what you don't know is a ninja.

TAIL AS BIG AS A KITE

Christmas is truly a magical time of year. The gentle kiss of heaven's snow on the frosted glass of our car windows. The sweet sounds of carols ringing their joyous melodies. The smell of that old drunk Santa blocking the entrance to Big Lots where I did all my Christmas shopping yesterday. Magical indeed.

But my house is more like the nightmare before Christmas—a real whine fest. But enough about me and my wife. The kids are even worse. They say nothing sweetens the proverbial eggnog of the holidays more than the laughter of children. It captures the essence of the Christmas spirit, carrying the whispers of eternal hope from generation to generation. The laughter of children is what makes all the humbug and hullabaloo of the holidays worth the money spent and sleep lost.

Or so I hear. I have four kids.

I love those little darlings so deeply that oceans could not contain my affection. For eleven months out of the year, they are my pride and joy. My bread and butter. My pickled eggs and nutmeg. But when December rolls around, something about my offspring changes. They are irritable. Demanding. Entitled. Someday I might even tell you about the changes. Annoying. Berating. Chiding. I could work my way through the entire alphabet if you want.

Christmas is kind of bittersweet for me. We all have our own unique reactions to the holidays. Some of us become giddy with joy, while others process the whole season with more restraint. Some of us face depression, while others seem to find emotional strength amidst the twinkling lights and beautiful holly. And some of us take naps. Some of us wear masks to hide the person we really are—and some of us paint those masks with purple stripes and glitter to match our lime-green leisure suits and studded feather boas—metaphorically, of course. Right, that's what I meant.

But I think my issues with Christmas come from my childhood. When I was about six years old, I secured a spot performing in my very first Christmas pageant at church. The church was filled with crowds of jolly people donned in their best reds and greens. Hearts were merry as families waited in anticipation to hear the songs of their sweet children ring out across the chilly night.

It was my artistic debut. I had no idea I would grow up to be an artist, but that Christmas play proved to be a humble beginning for Tiny Tim. I only had one line in one song. How hard could it be? The song was "Do You Hear What I Hear?" As scores of family and friends gathered together to celebrate the greatest gift God ever gave the world through the precious newborn life of his only begotten Son, I belted out a perfect melody of, "A child, a child, sleeping in the night . . . with a tail as big as a kite."

That's not how that song goes. People get mad when you sing about baby Jesus with a tail. However, I don't think I should be held fully responsible because the composer of that song must have been huffing myrrh or something at the time. Consider some of the other lines, even when sung correctly.

"Said the little lamb to the shepherd boy . . ." Really? Said the lamb? I think the shepherd boy's been out in the field a little too long. I wonder how that conversation went down anyway.

"Baaaaa!"

"Do what, Little Lamb?"

"Maaaaaa!"

"No way! We got to run and tell the mighty king!"

But it gets worse. Shep and Little Lamb set out to relay the four-legged animal's heavenly revelation to the mighty king. That must have been an awkward conversation with the guard at the door. "Let me get this straight, you and the lamb got a message for the king? Have you been eating sheep chips or something?"

But somehow, the message makes it through the approval process and once it is decoded, this is what the king learns about the Savior of the world. "A child, a child, shivers in the cold." What does the mighty sovereign suggest? "Let us bring him silver and gold . . ."

I'm no pediatrician, but I'm thinking that anyone in their right mind—shepherd, sheep, or otherwise—would know that a newborn baby lying in an animal trough developing hypothermia has a very specific set of needs. How about a blanket? How about some soup, for Christ's sake . . . literally. The child's shivering in the cold. Nah, throw some gold on him. He'll be fine. He's got pneumonia, but he's loaded. He's set up for life—if he can make it through the night, of course.

Gifts and animals—these were integral components of the original Christmas story. Maybe that's why these two themes keep coming up every Christmas around my house too. Once again, my daughter is begging for a puppy. A puppy? I can't stand animals. If I would have been Noah, it would be just you and me around here. You wouldn't be reading about any ark with hundreds of special rooms for all the critters. Nope. It would be a pontoon with a couple of Jet Skis. Wouldn't need no ark.

So Christmas or no Christmas, the Hawkins puppy is not happening. I can't stand dogs. Once again, I think my issues may stem from my childhood. When I was younger, my cousin had a vicious little poodle. Some people think poodles are so cute, but that dog was just a pit bull with a perm.

People are crazy about their dogs these days. If you ask me, some of them like their dogs just a little too much. They lose their sense of logic and reasoning. The other day, I walked up on this lady and her dog at the park. I was trying to be nice, so I started petting the dog and saying nice things about him. "Aw, he's a good boy. Such a good boy."

"She's a good girl!" the lady snarled at me and curtly responded. Oh, sorry. I didn't have time for an exam. It's not like the dog was carrying a pocketbook.

One of my friends lets his dog lick him in the mouth. When I begin gagging in protest, he says, "Come on, man! The dog's tongue is the cleanest part of his body." That may be the case, but when I drove up I saw him using it to clean the dirtiest part of his body. Your logic's a little flawed there, dog whisperer.

Still, the Christmas dog requests just won't stop. Knowing my aversion to poodles, my daughter has tried to sidestep me by claiming she now wants a dachshund puppy. I tried to reason with her. "Honey, I read dachshund puppies are terrible with children."

"You're terrible with children!"

"That may be true, honey, but Daddy doesn't pee on the carpet—well, just that one time. But that was before I knew Jesus, so that doesn't count at all."

Tweet Thought @timhawkinscomic
Out of the proper context, having an arrow shot through your heart by a flying baby would be horrifying.

Tweet Thought @timhawkinscomic
After using Chapstick I like to point at it and say, "You da balm!"

ONE CRAZY RELATIVE

I believe God made the human experience to be a shared experience. This is why each of us can relate to someone else's perspective. Somewhere out there right now, another person is doing exactly what I'm doing. What a crazy idea.

But there's something crazier than the truth of this concept, and so far I have never met a person who did not share at least one particular experience with me. Everyone out there has at least one crazy relative. If you cannot think of a crazy relative—yep, you are the one.

Recently our entire family got together to celebrate Christmas. We reminisced about the joys and heartbreaks of yesterday. We read the Christmas story aloud and prayed a prayer of thanksgiving for all the blessings we enjoy. We even sang a few carols together, letting the beauty of family ring out in our harmonies. The other 90 percent of the time we sat gazing into our smartphones.

Everyone who knows the joy of family knows exactly what happened next. We sat with our children and marveled as mounds of wrapping paper were viciously shredded and tossed about amidst shouts of jubilation. And yes, there was the occasional physical altercation over a gift one received that another jealously wanted for themselves. Such squabbles are commonplace when this level of immaturity abounds. And after all that, we let the kids open their gifts too. It was magical.

After the joyful mayhem had subsided, we lounged about with hot chocolate and wassail to reflect on the past year and make plans for the one to come. The conversation eventually led to the topic of taking a family vacation. Everyone was discussing the idea of heading off to Hawaii.

That was when crazy decided to rear her lovely head and begin speaking. My cousin chimed in with, "No way! I would never go to Hawaii."

"Why not?" I asked.

"Because they hate Americans." Let that line sink in for a minute before you read on.

"What are you talking about?"

She gave me a talk-to-the-hand look and confidently said, "Duh, Pearl Harbor. They hate us over there."

Oh yeah, we entered World War II because we attacked ourselves. I forgot about that.

But I guess crazy is genetic because it seems to rise up in other members of my family too. A few weeks after Christmas, it crept into my dad. We were over at Mom and Dad's house visiting and I accidentally locked my keys in my car—not to be confused with all those times I purposely lock my keys in my car. At any rate, I was pretty bummed about the situation and was about to call AAA to come help out . . . not to be confused with AA. That extra *A* is very important in moments such as these.

"Hi, I'm Tim . . . and I locked my keys in my car."

"Hi, Tim!"

But it was Dad to the rescue. "Son, you don't need to call anybody. I'll be right back." He walked into the house and came out straightening a wire coat hanger.

"What are you going to do there, MacGyver?" I jabbed. This is a man who has a toolbox wherein the only contents are an index card with a guy's number who knows how to fix stuff. But the joke was on me because I kid you not when I say he popped open that car faster than Nicholas Cage in any of his seventeen horrific and unwatchable movies about stealing cars. I don't exactly remember the titles of the films, but they are almost all cheesy and have something to do with speed. Titles like *Drive Fast, Drive Angry, Driving Miss Crazy, Grand Theft AutoCorrect*—the one where he plays a Microsoft employee who stumbles into a life of crime. It's a tale as old as time.

But movies aside, Dad rocked. I don't know if he used to steal cars as a kid or what, but I was legitimately impressed. Yep, that's my dad. The one who taught me how to field a ground ball. The one who taught me how to slam a forehand in Ping-Pong with an empty detergent box. The one who kept all of us kids safe during storms and defended our home from intruders. A suburban gladiator. And now he had proven himself to be "the man" once more.

Then he opened his mouth and ruined everything. "Timmy, here's what you do. Take this coat hanger. Put it in your trunk. That way you'll have it the next time this happens."

We were oh so close to a father-son moment that I could taste it. Turns out, the flavor was bittersweet. My sentiments about the whole thing could have easily been spoken (that is to say, overacted) by Nicholas Cage just after one of the nine one-eyed Mexican drug lord villains smoking huge stogies in one of his movies—any of his movies—narrowly missed crashing into his car for the eighth time.

"Close, señor, but no cigar."

Tweet Thought @timhawkinscomic
"Liar liar! Pants on fire!" Call me crazy, but I think lying is more forgivable than taunting someone with burning pants.

Tweet Thought @timhawkinscomic
If these walls could talk, I'd probably listen, but I wouldn't tell anybody I got my information from a wall.

TECHNOLOGY

Technology was supposed to make our lives easier, but I'm beginning to question whether or not that has happened. I will say this: it has made parenting easier. Just the other day I instructed one of my kids to come to me and he did not respond. He suffered the verbal consequences. "Look, you come upstairs when I text you! Do you understand what I'm saying? Don't you walk away from me when I'm talking to you. I will unfriend you, my friend. Don't think I won't do it. You're in big trouble, mister!"

But regardless of how we individually feel about texting, tweeting, or posting, we have to stop doing these things while we're driving. I mean seriously, is what we have to say so important that it is worth risking our lives over? It can wait—at least for a red light or gas station stop. This is a cultural trend that must be reversed.

Just last week, I was driving down the road minding my own business. This lady driving a black Toyota Land Cruiser pulled up beside me on a four-lane highway, and I could tell she was not paying attention at all to what she was doing behind the wheel. She was completely engrossed in composing a text message or a tweet or something. All I have to say is those must have been some very long hashtags— #excitedtobeendangeringeveryonearoundme #hollaatyogirl #YOLO.

Before I could honk to get her attention, she swerved into my lane, running me off the road into a ditch. I couldn't believe it. Thankfully, I was the only one in the car and the damage to my vehicle was superficial. It shook me up, though. This Formula 1 Female did not even stop to check on me or see if I was okay. She just drove on her merry way continuing to text, completely oblivious to the fact that anything had happened. The nerve of some people—I almost spilled my bowl of cereal on my lap. "Why don't you learn how to share the road, moron!" My spoon went flying out the window and I had to drive with my knees. Driving is hard enough as it is—especially when you're eating Chinese food while driving a stick shift. You have to have laser-like focus. No distractions. Please. Stop the texting.

You've got to pay attention when you're texting. Have you ever sent a text to the wrong person? I have. Recently I was sending an intimate text to my wife. It read, "I love you. I miss you. I want you." Send. Yep, I just sent that to my son's baseball coach. That's going to be awkward dropping him off at batting practice this week. They have autocorrect for composing texts in the present, but there is no auto-correct for after you send them. Oh if only there was—like a magic Wi-Fi angel who can intercept errant texts at the speed of light when such action is needed.

It's tragic really. We are just too dependent on technology. I don't know. I just feel like some of our technological advancements have gone just a bit too far. I was in Walmart the other day shopping for an anniversary present for my wife when I came across something called the Quattro. It's a razor for men that has four blades. Four. Now besides the obvious Spanish misspelling, I see another problem here. Four blades just seems a little overkill to me—and I mean that quite literally.

I get it. The first blade grabs the hair. The second blade grabs the hair a little lower. The third blade cuts off the hair at the root. One would think that at this point, the goal of shaving would have been sufficiently accomplished. But the Quattro pushes the limits of technology to a deeper level—down to the bone, to be exact. The fourth blade swoops in and takes out a chunk of your cheek about the size of a tea bag. I'm not sure a few tiny dots of toilet paper stuck to my face are going to help here. I'm just saying that when the package contains a release form and you need a pack of gauze after every shave, the razor may be overengineered just a skosh.

Perhaps the brilliant scientists who are pushing the limits of time and space over the Quattro should consider adding a fifth blade. Why not a hundred blades so I can shave my legs, chest, and face at the same time? Just take me out of my misery.

With great innovation comes great responsibility. I should know. I once created a potato gun that put my brother in the hospital. Like I said, he should have exercised more responsibility and ducked faster.

But much like so many of the issues we are dealing with in the modern health-care crisis, the folks down at Quattro should take a long look in their shaving mirrors, as foggy as they may be. As our capacity to do great things as a society continues to increase exponentially, we must constantly remember that just because we can do something does not mean we should. Come on, Quattro, drop one of the blades—lives are depending on it. And while you're at it, try running spellcheck every now and again and dropping one of those *t*'s too.

My culling of technology does not end with the Quattro conspiracy. I'm just sick of the way technology seems to enhance our laziness past the point of reasonability. Look, I possess a reasonable level of laziness. If I lose the remote control, the odds are very small that I will stand up and change the channel manually. What am I, an animal? If I were to stand that close to the television, can you even imagine what it would do to my eyesight? No, I will usually just stop looking and take a nap instead, thus waiting for my wife to find it the next day. See, that makes sense.

But some of this stuff just goes too far, even for me. It is nothing but lazy technology for the sake of laziness itself. Take, for instance, the electric toothbrush. Seriously America? Is brushing your teeth too strenuous an exercise to do manually? Were we getting carpal tunnel from the excessive motion? We should be ashamed. What's next— electric deodorant?

Makes one wonder why they put those rubber grips on tooth-brushes. Are you really brushing your teeth so fast that you need a little extra gription? "Yep, lost my grip and tomahawked another toothbrush through the drywall again today. I know I need to slow down, but these slippery suckers are just so hard to hold on to at the supersonic rate of speed necessary to fully clean and disinfect my incisors. If only there was an answer technology could provide."

Last year for Christmas, I received the laziest gift imaginable from my kids. It was an alarm clock that projects the time onto the ceiling. Seriously? Are we so lazy that we can't turn our heads the fifteen degrees necessary to see the alarm clock on the bedside table? Do you actually think a person this lazy would actually be setting an alarm anyway? "Yep, I need to get up by 11:00 a.m. or else I might miss *Judge Judy*—and then my day would just be shot. Got to leave extra time to brush and give myself a skin graft."

Tweet Thought @timhawkinscomic
I said "YOLO" to my Hindu friend and of course he disagreed.

Tweet Thought @timhawkinscomic
Giving someone a ride in my car always entails a mad dash clearing all the trash away from the passenger seat area.

EAT WHAT YOU WANT

My friends keep telling me to work out. I know it would probably help prolong my life span and whatnot, but I want those years to be worth living. You gotta let the game come to you. You can have your cake and eat it too. And you can eat others' unfinished cake out of the trash can at birthday parties. The world is your oyster—and you can eat that too. Listen, you lasted forty years. Eat what you want. You made it. Get creative.

The other day I ate some cheesecake and used a piece of bacon as a fork. And don't start judging me until you've tried it, my friend. It'll change your life. I could feel myself dying, but I've never felt more alive. My heart was fluttering like a hummingbird's wings. It was like I was in the X Games or something. Who wants a few extra years if they entail eating rice cakes topped with celery sticks? And wash it all down with a nice carrot—prune—muffasa juice cocktail. Never heard of a fruit called muffasa? Me neither, but I fully expect them to discover it before I'm in my eighties. I also fully expect it to taste as bad as it sounds.

And this ab craze is ridiculous. As a country, we're a thousand trillion dollars in debt, but we've got ripped abs. I don't need good abs. The only crunches I'm doing are of the Nestle variety. Besides, even if I did have shredded abs, I don't have anything to go with it—nothing to complement them. I mean, what good is a six pack when you have a hairy back? That'd be great if I were a centaur. You can ask your homeschool friend what a centaur is.

Listen, this is forty—and it is what it is. This is as good as I'm going to get. I'm not going to improve this. I've got a crooked nose, lopsided ears, pasty white skin, and varicose veins. My toenails look like Sun Chips, for crying out loud. What is that all about? You wake up one day and you have Ruffles on your feet. One day when I grace the streets of gold with my greasy potato toes, I'm going to pose the question of the ages: "Uh, Lord? Look at what's on my feet. Seriously? Why did you do that?"

"I thought it would be funny. Can I interest you in some french onion dip?" And then I can just imagine God laughing hysterically as the heavenly hosts join in pointing and jeering at my feet. I will admit, I have some weird ideas about heaven. Perhaps sarcasm is in heaven as it is on earth.

But down here, people are constantly trying to tell me what to eat all the time. Just yesterday, one of my friends was like, "Hey, man, you've got to try this new diet, man. It's like a thousand calories a day!"

A thousand calories? Toothpaste has like eight hundred calories. What am I going to do? Brush my teeth and throw down a couple Wheat Thins? That doesn't sound like the kind of life I want for myself or my children. What sort of people are we becoming—besides obese, I mean? Is obesity really that bad?

Okay, so they say it is. But they don't have to be so pushy about it. These days, they're trying to scare us with food. This has been going on since I was a kid. I can remember when they first began talking about the dangers of cholesterol. "Stay away from the cholesterol!" they would say in their spooky voices straight out of an episode of *Scooby-Doo*. These days, it's all about trans fats. This one is pretty scary sounding. "Trans fats! Keep the children away, there's a trans fat in the building!" Next thing you know, they'll be invoking trans fat evacuation plans, which sounds a lot like defecation. My mother will be thrilled.

I'm not anti-health; I'm just pro-taste. Must we be forced to choose when the standards by which these decisions are being made are as ever-changing as the underpants of those who pound daily prune smoothies with psyllium husks? I'm sick and tired of hearing one day about the dangers of eating kiwis only to hear the next day that kiwis are some super fruit that prevents cancer, heart disease, and athlete's foot—all in one seed-ridden fell swoop. Let me tell you, you haven't lived until you've felt the sensation of slimy kiwi squishing between your fungi toes. That was an awkward moment for my wife to walk in on. With my hand in the cookie jar—or my foot in the fruit bowl. You get the point.

But back to my heaven concept—which is a logical thought progression. If we, as a society, were actually honest with ourselves, we would admit that we really do not know what is good or bad for us. I think there will be quite a few surprises in store for these doctors and dietitians who led so many of us astray on these grilled goose chases from one nutritional fad to the next. Yep, heaven will be a real Come-To-Jesus meeting.

I can just envision one of the angels sitting down with me in heaven's cafeteria for lunch. As I gnaw on a raw piece of broccoli because I think it must be a heavenly food, I glance over to Gabriel only to find him eating a funnel cake dipped in Nutella dipped in cake batter. He looks back at me as he wipes the powdered sugar from his cheek and says, "Dude, what are you doing with that broccoli?"

"Um, we were told this was what we should have been eating the whole time on earth. I just figured it was appropriate for heaven to—"

He cuts me off, laughing hysterically. "Who told you that? Didn't God warn you about listening to false angels of lite?" Don't ask me how I know he spells the word *l-i-t-e*. This is my heaven fantasy, so give me a break. Gabriel downs a whole cupcake as he continues instructing me on the true nutritional value systems of the universe. "You should've been eating the trans fats. Those things are awesome. They cure everything. Yep, trans fats and boogers."

"I'm sorry, sir, but did you just say 'boogers'?"

"Yeah, bro, get a clue. God positioned those little slimy miracle pills right up there in a little holder by your mouth, you moron. When people on earth used to rant and rave about 'going green,' that's the green you should've been going. You've been flicking away your healing for years, man."

That's why kids have so much energy. They've been chugging boogs.

Tweet Thought @timhawkinscomic

Man does not live by bread alone. —Jesus

God appears as bread to the hungry. —Gandhi

You gonna eat that bread? —Buddha

Tweet Thought @timhawkinscomic

I'm surrounded by paleos, vegetarians, and vegans. I'm more of a "megan." It's where I eat what me wants again and again.

PROTECTIVE
PADDING

Okay, if I hear one more friend talk to me about working out, I'm going to punch somebody. Well, I'd punch them if I could muster the strength to do so. I will at least write them a strongly worded letter, or perhaps a text rife with miffed emoji. That'll show them.

Just yesterday, my friend Chris said to me, "You need to work on your body, man." No, I don't. I work out sometimes and this is it. This may look like fattiness to you, but I need this. I'm proud of this.

You see, I'm in my forties and I've got three boys now. What others call fat, I call protective padding. You need protection when you've got boys. The reality is that they're coming for you. Maybe not today. Maybe not tomorrow. But soon . . . and for the rest of my life. They are gunning for me and it's going to hurt. My house is like MMA every day.

The paradox is that when it comes to children, the pain they can inflict worsens as their age goes down. My oldest boy is sixteen years old. He's very athletic and works out regularly. He's got muscles and let's just say that he's proud of them. These days when we wrestle, I actually have to try.

He came home from working out the other day and said, "Hey Dad, let me punch you in the arm and see if you can take it." He must have been in cahoots with my wife on this one because it was a question with no good answer. Now, in any normal human situation, the idea of freely and intentionally allowing another person, regardless of size, to deliver an unabated punch straight to your arm, or to any body part, for that matter, would be completely asinine on every level. Ah, but this is not a normal human situation—and neither am I nor my family members anything resembling normal humans. This is fatherhood—the most abnormal paradigm imaginable.

So the simple concepts of self-preservation and the avoidance of pain in any dosage no matter how small, offered valid reasons to say no to my son's request. But then I contemplated the shame of such a reply. I have heard many people say that they have an angel on one shoulder and a devil on the other. But with me, it's not so much a devil, but rather a potbellied redneck coaxing me into making poor life decisions. "Shoot fire, Timbo! That boy's gonna clobber you, but you ain't no sissy face, are ya?"

Before me stood a human not yet fully developed into an adult who I helped to create. Sometimes we forget that though our children are tall now, there was a time when we were fully grown and they did not even exist. And when he did finally exist on the outside of the womb, he weighed less than ten pounds and eventually ate out of the dog bowl on a regular basis.

That sort of background information left me with little choice. What was I going to do, wimp out and ask the person who used to lie in my arms while filling his diaper to please not hit me because it might hurt? I would have lost what minute crumbs of dignity marriage and being in my forties has left in my life. No, the die was cast—and somewhere in a hospital, an actual cast was also about to be cast.

Mind you, this entire mental discourse raced through my mind in the course of about four seconds. He had no idea I was even bouncing it around in my head at all. All he heard were the foolishly confident words I fired back at him, "Sure, bud. Take your best shot."

Darkness. Blurriness. Crippling pain. Incontinence. A clown with a leaf blower.

I remember waking up on the floor. I never knew arm pain could render one unconscious, but apparently my son is an overachiever and had cracked the code on punch delivery. He has a real future in boxing. Or organized crime. Or being the stunt double in the no-doubt-soon-to-be-made third unsuccessful attempt at making a decent Incredible Hulk movie. "Hulk smash dad!"

Apparently I was hiding my medical emergency pretty well because my son just stood there towering over me while he looked at himself in the mirror hanging on the wall behind us. To my surprise, he said, "Dad, did you feel that?"

At first, all I could muster was a squeak. I did not know it was possible to knock the breath out of someone via the arm. Finally, my voice returned as I violently exhaled in agony, "*My dad* felt that, you moron. My contacts flew out when you hit me."

The only fail worse than my own was that of the full body fat suit I had spent so many late nights at IHOP building up for moments such as these. It did not do its job at all. It turns out there are not many benefits to obesity. Someone out there in the media should say something or write a book to warn people. Maybe I could write it under the pseudonym Sugarfree Leonard and entitle it *Truth Syrup: How Eating Pancakes Got Me Pancaked*.

As I said, the greatest mystery of the pain inflicted upon fathers by their children is that as their age goes down, the pain goes up. One would assume the converse to be true. One would be wrong. Dead wrong.

Thus my eleven-year-old walked into the room the other day and said, "Hey Dad, let me shoot you with my air-soft gun." Air-soft, eh? I had never even heard of an air-soft gun, but I was about to find out. It sounded a lot like a Nerf gun or something else soft—what with the word *soft* in the title. It sounded harmless enough, so I gave my permission for the proverbial firing squad to pull the trigger.

"Sure, son. Go ahead." He pulled the trigger and once again, I hit the floor in a heap. What was that rounded projectile traveling at? Two thousand feet per second? That was impressive. If ever an example of false advertisement existed, air-soft is your bad guy. You might as well advertise open-heart surgeries as sternum massages. Or maybe put up a billboard for an IRS audit, but instead call it free math tutoring. Or produce ridiculously raunchy television commercials for heart disease, but instead call it Hardee's. Wait . . .

Air-soft. Nothing airy or soft about that bad boy right there. Should've called it the Weltmaker. Daddy would've said no. The only thing airy or soft is the cloud you ride up into heaven after taking a kill shot to the neck from one of these demon dots. Air-soft is nothing but a pellet moving at the speed of light. You can shoot through an oil tanker with one of these things. It was like a woodchuck bit my bedonkadonk.

Though it seems impossible that the pain could worsen, I am fearfully aware that I have even younger children. Oh my soul, yes—even greater pain awaits you from the little guys. That's the worst: knowing the pain is coming, but not knowing when. It can keep a man up at night.

I was giving my little one a goodnight kiss the other night. It was such a sweet moment between father and son. He is so innocent. So helpless. So inquisitive. He began exploring and stroking my beard. "Daddy, Daddy. You have a beard!"

"That's right, sweetie. I do." A gentler moment has never existed on the planet. My heart was full.

"Daddy, I like your beard. It's very soft, Daddy."

"I know it is. Someday, you'll have a beard, too, and Daddy will teach you how to shave." That seemed to bring a depth of joy to his little heart beyond measure. Our journey as father and son just beginning to emerge. Who could know what adventures lay before us on the horizon of family and faith?

He continued to explore the contours of my face. "Daddy, is that a nose hair?" And that was when the greatest and most unexpected pain of my life suddenly overtook me. *Bink!* He ripped said nose hair from said nose hole, leaving me incapacitated in coughing and sneezing fits of rage. Such tiny fingers, yet such tremendous agony.

"Yeah, I think it was a nose hair."

"Are you crying, Daddy?"

"No, son, I'm just laughing. I think I just tasted a little blood in my throat." What was weird was that when he pulled the nose hair, my leg went flying up in the air. It's like they were connected. Subsequent attempts at reenactment have yet to yield the same conclusion.

My children have taught me so much about life and living, but no lesson has been more memorable than the sudden and lasting realization that nose hairs are connected to the brain stem. That's some new information they never taught me in health class, nor did anyone in our Lamaze classes ever prepare us for moments such as these. How could they?

"Listen, after your wife endures the greatest pain imaginable and you both experience the greatest joy imaginable, you're going to want to keep your nose hairs closely trimmed or else your offspring will attempt to mimic the ancient Egyptian mummification process by ripping your brain out through your left nostril. More donuts?"

I suppose there are no manuals for parenting. Perhaps color-coded warning labels or open-ended prescriptions would be just as helpful. One can dream.

But despite the pain they inflict, kids can be so sweet and creative. I was at my friend's house in Texas and his six-year-old son was playing in the dirt—which in Texas means he was playing in the yard. I walked up and asked him what he was doing, you know, just being friendly.

"I'm feeding this caterpillar to these fire ants."

I instinctively took a step back, wondering if I was speaking with the young Hannibal Lecter of insects. As he continued to probe, so did I.

"You don't say. Well, is the caterpillar dead?"

He looked up at me diabolically and flashed an eerie grin. "Not yet." That young pest predator was the inspiration for an original song I wrote a few years ago—from the perspective of a little boy. I wrote it mainly so people will stay safe out there, especially if they get invited to come play in the "yard."

FIRE ANTS

Hey, little caterpillar, such a pretty caterpillar.
I know that you're gonna be a beautiful butterfly someday.
I don't know if that's gonna happen, because . . . I have decided . . .

To feed you to the FIRE ANTS! The FIRE ANTS!
They're gonna eat you up, they don't care about you.
They're gonna eat you up now. Fire, fire, fire yeah!
Whoa! You're gonna die.

Hey there little birdy, you are so sweet.
I love you little birdy, love it when you tweet, tweet, tweet . . .
And you know I love it when you sing.
But I see that you have a broken wing,

So I'll feed you to the FIRE ANTS! The FIRE ANTS!
They're gonna eat you up, they don't care about you.
They're gonna eat you up now,
Fire, fire, fire yeah!

Tweet Thought @timhawkinscomic
Hope my teenage daughter likes the swimsuit I bought her. It's a full-body one-piece with a cape and working porcupine quills.

Tweet Thought @timhawkinscomic
"Dad, Levi called me an idiot."
"Levi, I told you never to say that to his face."

MOON MAN

Some people think I'm famous. That's pretty hilarious. Look, just because people come from miles around by the tens of thousands to laugh at me, that does not make me famous. Clowns at the circus have the same effect on people.

I'm nothing but a clown—a terribly handsome and immensely talented clown with a tour bus and a closet full of brightly colored hats with those extremely long feathers coming off of them like unfurled flags that say, "Look at me, I'm not a clown." Honestly, I'm the one laughing. My fans have absolutely no idea that I have absolutely no idea what I'm doing out here. I hope you never find out. Confidence is a valuable asset when you're a fraud.

Oh, but my wife surely knows the truth. There's no fooling her. She loves me exactly the same as she did before I changed my name from Stefan Colonblow to my stage name, Tim Hawkins. And by the way, the real name is pronounced "ste-FAHN coe-LAHN-blo." Emphasis on the "LAHN."

Get it right, please.

But the point remains that to my wife, I'm the same old Tim Hawkins I have always been. No number of DVD releases, satellite radio plays, or television appearances will change that to her. And I wouldn't have it any other way. I love the fact that we are the same people we were twenty years ago when we tied the knot. (We met as deckhands on a pirate ship.)

Sometimes I will return home from a weekend trip out on the road where things went incredibly well only to find that things at home with our four kids did not go so incredibly well. I have been tempted to spill the beans about the crowds of people who laughed hysterically at my new jokes, but the look on Heather's face has many times revealed that she is one second away from throwing a can of beans right at my adorable comedy head. So I just always say, "Eh, it went okay. Probably not nearly as exciting as what happened around here."

People will often walk up to my wife and say, "Oh my goodness! You must just love being married to Tim! I bet it is just a hoot. I bet you laugh constantly all the time. It must be a real riot!"

Though she smiles and nods, I can read her thoughts. *Oh, it's a riot all right. And nothing tops off the experience more than when my husband waltzes in and cracks a poop joke about the whole thing—even though here in the real world, poop is no laughing matter. Yep. A riot indeed. That's why I keep a canister of tear gas hidden under my bed. Mommy Riot Gear.*

I wonder if other men in history ever dealt with these kinds of issues? You have to admit that what I do is pretty uncommon. I recall a few other men who did uncommon things in their lifetimes as well—great things that impact the present and future of our world. Things that change the course of history and leave generations con-templating their influence for centuries to come. You know, stuff like what I do.

In my estimation, nothing tops that iconic moment forty-five years ago when we beat the Russians in the space race. In terms of inventions and accomplishments, I think we haven't done much of anything since then. Sure we have satellites in space that can read your license plate, take your blood pressure, and ascertain your favorite Starbucks drink. Computer memory compartments, which used to fill whole warehouses, now comfortably fit into our pockets—even though instead of using them to solve complicated algorithms or improve world hunger, we mostly use them to post Instagram photos of things like dogs face-planting on Slip 'N Slides or selfies of shirtless eighth-grade boys after football practice looking like they don't know they are photographing themselves. You know, important stuff.

But if you think about it, the greatest thing we have ever done was to put a man on the moon. *We put a guy on the moon.* Well, I guess we didn't do it. But some guy did. Man, I would hate to be that guy when it was time to go home and take out the trash. That's some pressure right there. I bet his wife has used a certain verbal technique on that guy a time or two.

"Hey mister man on the moon, you forgot my birthday again! Hey, Larry Lunar, you think you could put a dish away every once in a while? They didn't teach you that in rocket science class? . . . Hey Captain Outer Space, this is how we earthlings put the cap back on the toothpaste: T-minus 10, 9, 8, 7 . . ."

No doubt on countless occasions he tried to use the fact that he innovated the whole moon landing thing as an excuse, but his wife was having no part of that. After work, he probably wanted to take a nap every now and again. He starts to lie down and she starts in.

"Why are you tired again?"

"Look, I put a man on the moon today!"

"Oh really? Let's see . . . did I 'put' anything of interest today? That's right. I put away clean clothes for four hours. I put up those curtain roads you should've hung four weeks ago. I put off my hair appointment to pick up your mother for her hair appointment. I put up with a ten-year-old with an attitude, a five-year-old who put a soap bar in the toilet, and a two-year-old who somehow put a half a bottle of ketchup in the cat's rear end. So forgive me if your little nap makes me feel a little put out!"

Put that in your pipe and smoke it, Blast-off Boy.

Tweet Thought @timhawkinscomic

Whoever wrote the song "Easy Like Sunday Morning" never took his kids to church on a regular basis.

Tweet Thought @timhawkinscomic

Good friends are like fine wine. That's why I keep mine locked in the cellar.

CHRISTIANESE

I am so blessed to get to travel to a diversity of different churches. Some people out there in the nonreligious world probably look down on me for spending my time in churches, but the joke is on them—church people are the funniest people on the planet. They give me endless amounts of material week in and week out.

I get annoyed when certain people try to act like all Christians are the same. Nothing could be further from the truth. Christianity, by biblical definition, is as diverse as the human body in terms of different parts and their functions. And since much of the living I make involves making fun of the sights, sounds, and smells of the human body, the church body is a temple rife with comedic potential.

I've been to some very cool churches. Churches with innovative personalities. Community-minded missions. Global impact. A sense of humor about life, faith, and family. The church is a great place to learn stand-up comedy as opposed to doing comedy in a club. Stage time at a club is hard to come by, whereas a youth leader will give you hours to hone your survival skills on a Wednesday night or Sunday morning in front of a crowd of teenagers, many of whom live by the mantra "What Would Jesus Don't."

Believe me, I've had some church experiences that were much more frightening than any club I've been to. You won't have anybody cussing you out and throwing beer bottles at you—but without all that beer, neither will they laugh if it isn't funny. And I have had a hymnal chucked at me and a few plastic communion cups whiz by my head during a performance. My toughest audience was at a middle school lock-in. Four hundred Beavis and Butthead types hyped up on pizza and Dr. Pepper. At one point I heard someone yell, "Give us Barabbas!" Tough crowd.

I've also been to some pretty messed-up churches. I do not say this to offend anyone—besides, anyone offended by this is probably the person I'm talking about anyway. I call that a comedic Double Bonus. But the truth is, we are all flawed and each church has to find its way through the maze of faith, community, and culture.

I think the funniest thing about churches is the language. It is a dialect that people outside the church would need a translator to understand. "Bless God, brother—if you want to head from the foyer on down to the fellowship hall, you'll see one of our ushers (they're the ones in the gold jackets) and they will get you a bulletin with a complete list of Life Groups, intercessory prayer groups, upcoming potlucks, and access to the church-wide prayer chain." Prayer chain? Is that what they use down in the prayer dungeon to keep people from escaping? It is no wonder so many new visitors often "escape" from our congregations before we ever get a chance to know them—they don't speak Christianese. Which gives me an idea about a new Rosetta Stone offering.

That's where I come in. I have spent many years studying the language of the modern church. They say that the best way to learn a language is to immerse oneself in a culture. Well, I have been baptized by immersion into this one—and as the theological reader will catch, I prove my own point. However, I also have no problem with sprinkling, religiously or otherwise, I suppose. Make your own conclusions.

Nevertheless I believe I can really help those immigrating into the church world understand how to navigate their way through our "customs" and get a decent grasp of what's going on. Hey, at least there are no metal detectors or cavity searches in our churches—well, that I know of. If you walk into the foyer and see a TSA agent handing out bulletins, I'd catch the tram back to the parking lot. Hey, we want to build deep relationships, but not that deep.

Most of the standard words or phrases are actually pretty easy once you get the hang of them. "Brother" and "sister" are ones you hear in a lot of churches. They are simply expressions of affection between Christians. Though I know they have been overused and are often considered to be antiquated and traditional, the terms are actually very cool because they denote family—and that is what Christianity really is all about. It is a family of faith with one Father and many children.

So though they may sound weird and can certainly be so overused that people stop treating each other like siblings in the sense of a permanent relationship defended at all costs, "brother" and "sister" can be a pretty cool thing.

It is also the Christian version of what most of us do when we can't remember someone's name that we most certainly should know. Out in the workplace or at a restaurant, we get by with a handshake and a "Hey man," or "Dude, it's been a long time." We might even throw in "buddy," "chief," or even the antiquated "partner." But in church? All you need is the trusty old "Hey brother. How's the sister doing?" It should be noted that such a sentence as I just used could cause trouble because in this case, the subject of the sentence could be interpreted as the man's wife or the man's biological sister. Again, immerse yourself in culture and you'll get the hang of it.

Now, for the extreme newbies, there are a few words or phrases that you should be warned about. On the surface, they sound so nice. So inviting. So spiritual. But beware. They are not what they seem. Many a new Christian has succumbed to the sirens and found themselves in a world of hurt over it.

For example, the phrase "servant's heart." It sounds so nice. It appears to be the ultimate compliment plucked straight from the branches of the Sermon on the Mount Tree. Note: that was a Churchonian reference. There is no actual tree called the Sermon on the Mount Tree. Tree of Life. Tree of Knowledge of Good and Evil. Even references to trees of righteousness in Isaiah. Such an expression like this is a great example of how Christians add metaphor to religious imagery. Just keep good notes and you'll get the hang of it.

But back to the servant's heart. Though on the surface there would appear to be no greater honor than to possess a spirit of servitude that is so evident that people could identify it just by your actions, you must know it is a trap. You see, when someone says to me, "Tim, you just have a real servant's heart," I go running for the doors. You should too. Or you can throw them off with, "And you have a real giver's appendix." Or perhaps, "You have the ankles of a provider." That should shut them up in a Christian way.

This is especially true if said words are spoken within the confines of the fellowship hall. Note: the fellowship hall is a multipurpose room mostly used as a Christian cafeteria; except unlike a secular cafeteria, everyone is generally required to bring their own food and if anyone is wearing a hairnet, it is because of misguided fashion reasons rather than health code requirements.

It should also be stated that such a gathering in which people are required to bring their own food is called a potluck. *Potluck* being a word that only exists in the church and simply means "food share." But trust me, much of the food brought to a potluck will not make you feel very lucky, which I guess is fitting since many Christians do not believe in luck at all, even though they constantly use the word in common greetings such as "good luck." But if you ask them about luck, they will say that nothing happens by chance—unless it is a potluck, which is a lot like a lottery in which the odds are good that someone will get salmonella. But don't call it a lottery because they also don't believe in gambling. Okay, this is getting too complicated. Focus on the servant's heart.

If someone ever tells me that I have a servant's heart, that just means they want me to start stacking chairs. "Servant's heart" means you're a pushover and a loser. Don't fall for it. They have stacks of chairs just waiting for people with "servants' hearts." I'm not saying to not be a servant or to actually have a servant's heart; I am merely helping you discern the language so you will not fall victim to common Churchonian colloquialisms.

"You've got a servant's heart, brother."

"No, you start stacking, Pastor! I got stuff to do."

The way people talk about their church is also a part of the language—it's like a code. If you hear someone say about a certain church something to the effect of, "I love it there . . . they have great music," please do not misinterpret them. Their church may indeed have great music, but what they actually mean is, "The preaching there really stinks." Conversely, if they say they love the preaching, that means the music stinks. If someone says, "I love it here because no one judges me and I can be who I want to be," you're at a bar. You've mistaken neon lights for stained-glass windows, brother.

You might also hear expressions like, "God gave me this," or "God gave me that." Please don't get me wrong or think me insensitive. I certainly believe that God inspires and speaks to his people—that is, he gives us stuff. But sometimes, we blame God for stuff he never gave us.

A lady will take the stage to sing in church and will say, "God gave me this song." And then she will proceed to actually sing the song and you will be thinking to yourself, *Maybe you should give it back. Before this moment, I have never dry heaved from listening to something, but maybe God didn't want you sharing that one, buttercup. Hide it under a bushel? Yes.*

God gave it to you? No, he didn't. Just start stacking chairs because that was horrible. And if God did happen to give it to you, something went horribly awry in the transition phase between heaven and earth, if you know what I mean. Don't feel bad. We have all been there. It is a part of being in the community of faith. You will survive.

And beyond the language, there are other customs you must prepare yourself for. At my church, the pastor always makes us hold hands across the congregation. I can't stand that. I have ADD and when the hand holding starts, you can bet your bottom dollar that I am no longer thinking about the prayer. I'm thinking about the person I'm holding hands with. *Man, this dude's hands are huge! I think he's got an extra finger or something. What is that? Is that a mole or a Milk Dud?*

Ew! I don't know if I'm sweating or if he is. Finish the prayer already before I catch a disease from Chewbacca man over here.

And finally, there is a certain Churchonian tradition everyone must know if they are to survive the hand holding that is inevitable among churches of all kinds. While you are holding hands and you finally hear the "amen" you have so been longing for, you or your prayer partner will give a little short squeeze. It doesn't matter who initiates. It can be either. I call it the "Amen Squeeze." It is the universal signal to let go and nonchalantly begin wiping those puddles of sweat from your hands onto your jeans in lieu of retrieving the hand sanitizer from your wife's purse.

It is a beautiful moment of community and cleansing, but try not to make it obvious.

Tweet Thought @timhawkinscomic
When my Christian friend copies music and gives it away, he doesn't call it piracy. He calls it a burnt offering.

Tweet Thought @timhawkinscomic
I've noticed the people most uptight about smokers and drinkers don't really have a problem with gluttony and gossip.

SMARTER THAN A FIFTH GRADER

I am fairly offended by the television show *Are You Smarter than a 5th Grader?* The insinuation this show is not so subtly making is that most American adults are not necessarily smarter than their fifth-grade counterparts. And the reasoning behind said intelligence evaluation? Basically, it's all based off of a few trivia questions. I find that entire premise itself to be trivial. Pun intended.

Now, I'm not claiming to have won any intelligence contests lately. I say lately because the last time I actually entered an intelligence contest was like seven years ago. It was pretty easy to sign up. I just had to send this guy two thousand dollars and answer some pretty tough questions from memory. They were mainly about my family history and some of my personal information—stuff like my social security number and whatnot. I don't like to brag, but I aced it. The guy even sent me a framed certificate that now proudly hangs in the new office I built after we declared bankruptcy due to a random identity theft.

You think a fifth grader could do all that? I doubt it. Who are smarter now?

That's my problem with this show. It just doesn't take into account all the issues of life that cannot be quantified by simple trivia. Sure, you might know the identity of the fourth president of the United States. You might know how many amendments there are to the Constitution. You might even know the capital of Washington DC. (I always struggled with that one.) But trust me, these things do not make you smarter than an adult.

There are a vast array of things that normal parents deal with day in and day out that would send fifth graders spiraling back to their potty training days before they could say "Jeff Foxworthy." Maybe the reason the adults on the show often cannot answer the same questions as the fifth graders is that their brains are completely clogged up with all the issues they are dealing with every day with their own fifth graders at home. We're just lucky these adults can find their way to the television studio without stopping in every alleyway along the road to find a corner to cry in. I find the parental fetal position is less humiliating when you can assume it in more private locations.

In this respect, the whole game show is rigged. Can we really expect a parent to have the mental fortitude for such an exercise in futility? All right fifth grader, why don't you try buzzing in with a correct answer on this little question—which is "child's play" for any parent out there:

Child A and Child B are fighting over Child A's toy. The first parental variable is that there is no way to actually know which child, whether Child A or Child B, was playing with the toy initially. It is also quite possible that Child A was just being a control freak as you cannot recall a time when he has played with the toy in question in the last two years. As they are fighting over the toy of ill repute, said object becomes a projectile and flies out of their greasy little mitts, hitting Child C in the face. Child C is now screaming and bleeding. Without using excessive narcotics and/or immoral levels of violence, what is the correct parental response to the situation? Yeah, solve that, fifth grader. And please write in complete sentences.

Oh, and here's a bonus question. You just got laid off from your job and while you are dealing with the crisis involving Child A, B, and C, your wife calls to tell you that Child D is on the way.

Pencils ready, Lunchable Boy.

Besides, any parent knows that fifth graders, no matter what their level of trivia knowledge, are not poster children for common sense. Or uncommon sense, for that matter. I have heard more than one teacher make the comment that there is no such thing as a stupid question. Well, I beg to differ. Obviously those teachers don't actually have children of their own. My kids ask questions all the time that prove they are not, in fact, smarter than the average parent—or even the average tree squirrel.

Any adult who has ever spent excessive time in a car with children on a road trip knows that there is a fine line between good mental health and insanity. It's called the space between the front seat and backseat. The questions are beyond reasonable, but none drives the driver crazier than, "Hey Daddy, are we there yet? Are-we-there-yet-are-we-there?"

I always try to answer with gentle wisdom. "The car's still moving, moron. Here's a rule of thumb: when the trees stop doing that moving thing outside the window, the eagle has landed, Ferdinand Magellan. You want to leave daddy alone for a few hundred miles?"

But no matter how much gentle fathers try to reason, the question continues to be asked. "Are we there yet?"

"Yeah, we're there. Daddy likes to get someplace and then just keep on driving."

I'm not trying to act as if children are the only ones who ask stupid questions. Certain adults are not immune to the outbreak of ignorance. My dad used to ask stupid questions on road trips. I can remember being halfway to Florida when I piped up with a reasonable request. "Daddy, I have to go to the restroom. Can we stop sometime soon?"

Dad's response was, "Number one or number two?"

Really? What difference does it make? Pull over, you weirdo. What I'm feeling internally is not exactly easy to gauge. I don't know, it could be one and a half? It suffices to say that I'm feeling some tension down there. So just pull over, Jeff Gordon, or these fake leather seats are going to be a different color in about thirty seconds. Got it, Captain Question?

One time I said, "Dad, I *really* have to go to the bathroom."

I kid you not, he replied with, "Lie on your side." Okay man, I know that's not going to work. Now only half of me has to go. Thanks for the bladder infection, Father of the Year.

I even had teachers who occasionally descended into a fifth-grade wisdom. One day, I brought a piece of candy to school with me. My teacher asked me, "Did you bring enough for everybody?"

Well, let's see. I'm a kid, not a caterer. So no, I did not bring enough for everyone. Honestly, I did not see any of these bozos help me mow the lawn to pay for this candy. So negative on that, Karl Marx. And that's why I have somewhat adapted the common expression a bit to reflect a more Hawkinsonian perspective.

There are no dumb questions—only dumb people.

Tweet Thought @timhawkinscomic
My kids need to realize that Chick-fil-A always gives them one too many waffle fries. And I can't have that. Sometimes two.

Tweet Thought @timhawkinscomic
Amazing that I've made it this far in life; without knowing when to use a semicolon.

SNICKALOAF

Years ago, there were theories abounding about those who circled little buildings that were donned with arches. Golden arches, to be exact. People even made documentaries and what-not about the dangers of McDonald's food. One guy decided to eat McDonald's every meal of every day for a month to see what happened. Literally, his physician told him he was going to die.

Well, sure he almost died. Something as wonderful as McDonald's is not made for such copious consumption. His experience was a lot like those shows where people win the lottery and it ruins their lives. They are just not equipped for that level of extravagance. It changes everything. Such is the case with McDonald's. It's just like *The Message* Bible says, "Man cannot live by fries alone." Amen to that.

In case you can't tell, I have a problem. Now, I know what you're thinking: *You may need to narrow that down a bit, buddy.* Don't get cute with me, imaginary voice of the reader. I will close this book right now and you will be left to guess how it ends.

I'm just kidding. I have no control over your ability to keep turning the pages of this book—nor its ending, for that matter. I'm making this stuff up as we go, but my money's on the butler in the library with the candlestick.

Please try to focus here. My initial point is that I just love food so much. And the thing is, food keeps getting better and better, as we old people can attest to. Again, there used to be theories about the addictive nature of McDonald's food among kids. I think that's ridiculous.

Everyone knows the first Happy Meal is free—it's the adult meals that really get you hooked.

In fact, I have started ordering multiple combo meals using the combination of their numbers to guess what my waist size will be the next time I go to purchase pants. It's a fun game, but it's not like it's life or death—I mean, until you die from it.

Nuance.

Anywho, last week I ordered a number seven and a number eight—it's like I'm playing Rhino Roulette (and I'm the rhino) every time I go to Old Navy. "Come on, lucky size seventy-eight! Daddy needs a new pair of corrective orthopedic boots before he slips off into this coma."

I tell my kids that they think McDonald's is great now, but they should just wait—it becomes magnificent. In fact, it's almost too magnificent. I know God says that no temptation comes without a way of escape, but have you ever been in the drive-through line with five cars both in front of and behind you? That way of escape exists, but it will require some major body repair, which ironically, is what will also be required if you stay in line and eat what you've ordered. The way our world is going, I say choose the option with the best insurance coverage.

The other day, I asked my wife, "Honey, why is McDonald's just so good?"

"I think they use MSG," she replied.

"I think they're using crack." I have never been able to prove it because I don't have a laboratory, the proper equipment, or intelligence, but I think there is definitely a breakdown of nugget integrity when it comes to those little meat shrapnels.

Confession is good for the soul—especially when other people are doing the confessing and you get to laugh at them. But truthfully, I wonder if anyone else out there shares my shame—the shame of attempting to successfully navigate a McDonald's drive-through experience with arteries unscathed—that is, by ordering and eating something healthy.

You pull up behind a car ordering in front of you and begin psyching yourself up for what's to come. You can do this. You begin audibly pep talking yourself with the words, "I'm going to get a grilled chicken salad and a bottle of water. A grilled chicken salad and a bottle of water. Grilled chicken salad and . . ."

"Welcome to McDonald's. Can I help you?"

"Yeah, give me a number one. Biggie-sized with some gravy on it and a couple of cinnamon rolls. And a defibrillator and a doctor's appointment. And can you dip the bag in chocolate? Can you do that? Oh, and a grilled chicken salad and a bottle of water."

It is a sting I know well, but there is no denying the addiction. In fact, nothing overjoys my soul more than stumbling upon extra fries in the bottom of the McDonald's bag. That just makes my week. It's like I have already engorged myself in vats of saturated fat, but then the delightful ride keeps going. My heart cries, "It's not over. I found some under the napkins! This, right here, is truly a happy meal—and I could not be any happier."

My food issues only begin at McDonald's. I'm not sure these issues have a final destination (besides the operating room), but they certainly love to vacation in Candy Land. And I don't mean the children's board game. More like a bored game compared to what I'm talking about. My version of Candy Land is one that involves actual candy. Actual gingerbread people. An actual ice cream sea. It's a magical place where dreams come to life and healthiness comes to a delightfully sticky conclusion. I envy my kids because though they think candy is good now in their childhood, it gets so much better. They have so much to look forward to.

However, I am no fool—I don't care what the online personality tests repeatedly say. There is some bad candy out there. I have vivid memories of getting together with my friends and venturing out in full costume begging for free candy. Pulling up a chair to join a genuine Oktoberfest. A free-for-all that was gloriously free for all. That's the one truth about taking candy from strangers—it's delicious. It brings tears to my eyes just thinking about it.

At any rate, I remember trick-or-treating on Halloween. We kids would set out to seek-and-find the most delectable delights one could fit into my dad's pillowcase (which I had borrowed on my way out the door despite the fact that it smelled like it had been steeped in a malodorous stew of Old Spice and a fart). These days, kids sport these fancy plastic pumpkin pails and whatnot. That's overkill if you ask me. The key to becoming king of Candy Land is maximum obesity with minimum investment.

Most times, we were successful at gaining good candy. Chocolate of any sort is a proven winner. Lollipops. Even candy corn, although it is an acquired taste—you know, like sushi or Brussels sprouts or spray paint.

But not all candies are created equal. On the great free fall that leads to obesity, one can eventually hit the absolute rock bottom of candy collection. Once, I opened up my bag and the lady dropped in what seemed to be a cellophane-wrapped moon rock. I lacked the subtlety that adulthood has now produced in my reactions. I was aghast and asked, "What is this?"

The lady mustered up the best smile she could, despite my adolescent rudeness. "That's a popcorn ball, sweetie. I made it myself."

"Well, then you need to eat it yourself!" I have no pride regarding what happened next, well except for the velocity at which I pitched that poisonous gob of hardened goo back at her. Some professional baseball players have built their careers on pitches like the curveball or the knuckleball. That night, I became the master of the popcornball.

I also remember receiving wax lips in my candy bag. We didn't know what it was, but we ate it anyway. It had no flavor whatsoever. And it would continue to just get bigger and bigger as you chewed it. Makes sense, really. We all want to chew inedible tasteless wax shaped like lips. Great call, candy-making companies. Great call indeed.

Then there were those wax bottles that contained a mysterious liquid on the inside. What was that? Power-steering fluid? "This is fantastic. I can feel it burning my esophagus all the way down. Ninety-nine bottles of flavored cyanide on the wall . . . ninety-nine bottles of flavored cyanide . . . Take one down, pass it around . . . call 911 stat!" No wonder we have all these health problems later in life. We drank battery acid out of wax for the first decade of our lives.

Horrible candy leaves such an impression. I recall the brown taffy in the orange wrapper. It tasted like peanut butter and hair. Nevertheless we had to eat that stupid candy. Why? Because your dad always ate all the good candy. You get home after four hours of a successful hunt. Toss your bag of booty on the kitchen table. Go upstairs to change into something more comfortable. Come back downstairs and Dad's in a sugar coma on the couch. Twix wrappers strewn all over his body. Thanks a lot, Pops.

I think it's hilarious what they consider to be candy these days. I went to purchase candy at the store the other day and I came across a bag of mini-Snickers. They were labeled as a "fun size." Come on. That ain't fun. A true fun size would be a whole bag of Snickers all jammed and melted together. We could label that bad boy a Snickaloaf. It's a piece of cake—literally, people could slice up their Snickaloafs and serve them up like pieces of cake. You and your need for metaphors. Sheeze.

Snickaloafs could become a magical holiday tradition that would change our way of life. Little Snickalelves at the South Pole scurrying around preparing their chocolate/caramel/peanut confections to distribute to little boys and girls around the world, all while awaiting the arrival of good old St. Snick. We'll hang our empty Snickaloafer stockings over the fireplace.

Snickalween!

It's a marketing breakthrough. No popcorn balls. No flavored poison in wax containers. Just simple candy logs of disproportionate goodness—that are horrible for you. And the promise of a brand-new year right around the corner.

If the fates allow.

Tweet Thought @timhawkinscomic

If Conway Twitty ever tweeted something witty about trick-or-treating, it would be a really witty Twitty trick-or-treat tweet.

Tweet Thought @timhawkinscomic

Candy hearts: the romantic message should take your mind off the fact that you're eating chalk.

KID-FRIENDLY

My travels around this country are actually not about comedy. This journey is really all about people. Without people, there is no laughter. Without laughter, there is no show. Try being all alone and writhing around on the floor imitating the sound a constipated llama might make. People would call that crazy.

I just call that Wednesday.

But the truth is that without people being present to laugh, I would simply be a seriously disturbed man with crazy stories, expressions, and viewpoints. Put it this way. I would be an extremely funny customer service representative. But because of the people who watch my YouTube videos, buy my DVDs, or come to my shows, things are different. I am a seriously disturbed man with crazy stories, expressions, and viewpoints. See the difference?

But in all honesty, I love people. I think they need to laugh. To feel the reality of a life lived apart from all things heavy. There is a lighter place we can live. Not just flippant or immature. But a place of freedom.

So it excites me when families come to my shows, because I love the fact that they get to laugh together. I never want my comedy to alienate anyone—adults, teens, children, animals, aliens—anyone really. See what I mean? I probably just offended some distant planetarian pilgrim out there in space somewhere because I used the term *alienate*. I can just see some alien mother with three kids and three eyes reading this journal and throwing it to the floor in anger.

"Fo'j. Quit watching that stupid cosmic bowling and come look at this!"

"Just a second, Qaeboqae, Thor is bowling a perfect game going into the eighth frame."

"Don't make me go all 'Kahn' on you, Fo'j. Get over here and read this now!"

"Yes, dear. What is it about this time? Another moon landing letter from the homeowners association?"

"No, it's this book by Tim Hawkins. Although generally delightful as a person and the most hilarious humanoid in the universe, he has just gone too far this time. He used the A-word. Why can't people stop marginalizing us just because we're aliens?"

Tragically unnecessary, really. And as Fo'j aims his gamma ray cannon at earth in an effort to vaporize us over a few words from my book, he fails to realize that my goal was never to alienate—I mean, make anyone feel distant from anyone else because of my comedy. I want comedy to bring us all together. But it does make one wonder what aliens call it when they want to describe the same issue. "I don't mean to 'earthlinginate' anyone here at our small group tonight, but this casserole sucks. Kahn!"

This political correctness stuff is tough. Darn it, I probably just offended a politician. Oh well, I guess if you're going to make an omelet, you'll have to break a few eggheads.

However, my dream is that every member of an average nuclear family—even if said alien family is pointing their advanced nuclear weapons at our planet as we speak—would enjoy my shows. And my journal, for that matter—although this does feel a little intrusive. I want children to laugh. Teens to roll their eyes as they text on their iPhones, but actually be texting, "I am so LOL'ing right now at this old dude." I want adults to laugh so hard that they lose control of their bladders. Hey, it happens.

So there are times that I address certain topics that seemingly are not "kid friendly." These are delicate waters, which I realize is not a thing, but it just sounds less heavy than saying dangerous waters. Dangerous waters would indicate that I know that talking about these things crosses some unspoken line of appropriateness, when my point is actually that the line is okay to cross if we cross it together in jest and stay within the boundaries of wisdom and unity. Therefore, these waters are not dangerous. They are delicate, just like my hands.

And I would like to pause to extend a special thank-you to my inner monologue for sharing that previous paragraph with both the reader and the writer. I have to work on thinking without talking—or talking without thinking. Or walking and chewing gum. Or washing my socks. So much to do.

But concerning families at my shows, I do tell jokes about alcohol. I know, you may be shocked. All humans are susceptible to the effects of alcohol if they ingest it. It is processed in their liver and released into their bloodstream producing all kinds of varying symptoms. Dizziness. Silliness. Tipsyness. Voting Democrat. Some people become belligerent and mean-spirited, saying and doing things they would never do if they were not under the influence of a foreign substance in their body.

But I have been shocked to learn that there is an entire contingency of people who experience some of these symptoms without actually having ever taken even a single sip of alcohol. It is a medical anomaly. I see it every time I do a show and simply mention the word *liquor.*

I think I have some special gift of transferring liquor into people's bloodstream via telekinesis. I should mention that for the most part, this only occurs in churches, so the phenomenon is confined mostly to a faith-based demographic. This is a group I am happily a part of, though I've never experienced this sensation for myself. I'm just saying that my observations are that this telekinetic "buzz" seems to mostly occur in places where peoples and steeples are in close proximity to one another.

The symptoms? Most people (not steeples) start getting silly and begin laughing. This is to be expected. Then there is the occasional vomiter. Funny, but not fun to clean up. At least it usually gets the others laughing even more. It's like a domino effect, but instead of dominoes falling down, someone sprays the crowd with their own stomach bile. What a hoot.

But despite all this fun, there are some who instead become belligerent and fold their arms in protest—just from an innocent acknowledgment that alcohol even exists. I'm not squirting Vodka into the crowd with a Super Soaker. I haven't done that since college.

But what hypocrisy to think that these offended ones are themselves under the telekinetic influence of the very thing they hate so much. How can I tell they are starting down the path of getting pejoratively plastered? Well, they begin staggering out of their seats and stumbling for the door. When this happens, I ask the ushers to detain them and commandeer their keys.

They may be furious at the moment, but they always thank me later—actually, I'm still waiting for a thank-you. Instead, I keep getting this hate mail. Potato-Potahto, I suppose. But keeping them off the road is worth it because that's just what we need in this country, more DWSs: Driving While Self-righteous. Nope, not on my watch.

I want people to stay and hear me out on this one because my point in mentioning alcohol is never to encourage its consumption. Quite actually, the opposite is true. I especially want the kids in the room to know—no joking around—that they absolutely do not need drugs or alcohol to have a good time. Period.

Have you seen the way things are going in this world? And as I get older, I know how things are going in my own brain. Last week, I couldn't remember where I left my list of things to remember. Now that is a vicious cycle from which there is no escape.

So see, kids, we need your brains—and we need them fully functional. God has given you a wonderful brain. When you think about it, your brain is a computer made out of meat. That's pretty cool. You have a meat computer installed in your skull. Don't jack it up with substances you don't need—that might make it freeze up or even crash. You are more important than that.

You have to learn to stand up for yourself and be confident in your decisions before people try to influence you—because throughout your life, they will indeed try. The biggest mistake you can make is to wait until the actual moment of decision to try to make a decision. Make the decision now so that when those moments arise, there will be no decision left to make—only a follow-through of what is already decided in your heart.

I'm not the only one out there trying to help people make these good decisions, and I appreciate the efforts of others. However, I have to be real with you. Sometimes the only thing worse than drugs are anti-drug slogans. No offense, but it's no wonder we have a drug abuse epidemic in our country. I think that sometimes people may be taking drugs just to numb the pain they are experiencing from enduring anti-drug campaigns.

Take, for instance, "Hugs not Drugs." Come on, is that how we roll? We just find a word that rhymes with a vice and we think we've won the war on drugs? I can do that all day. How about "Think Don't Drink"? Boom. I just saved a nation.

I could keep going, but the message gets a bit diluted in places. "Mime Not Crime." Less expected, but equally effective. Trust me— most mimes will not have to worry about being offered drugs. Or alcohol. Or dates with the opposite sex.

"Train a Seal, Don't Steal." This one's huge with the under-reported seedy underworld of organized crime at SeaWorld. Those guys really make otters you can't refuse, if you know what I mean. And if you don't like it, you'll be swimming with the fishes, if you know what I mean. Honestly, that's what I mean—it's delightful fun.

"Put Down the Crack, Eat a Big Mac." Is there actually that much of a difference between crack and the Big Mac? Both are extremely addictive. Both destroy your health. Both have onions and a special sauce. I should probably note that I have never done crack and I really don't know much about how it works. "Hey, I smell onions. Has someone been doing crack in here?"

But my point is that these slogans are just not working. Who's our drug czar these days, Dr. Seuss? "I will not take these drugs with Spam. I will not sell them to a lamb. I will not take them, dealer man."

I wish these program leaders would take a page out of my good friend Steven Curtis Chapman's book. That guy wrote the song about drugs and alcohol. He has won multiple Grammys. You have probably heard this song at many weddings or on the radio. It has touched the hearts of millions. It is called "I Will Be Here."

Actually, I've not been satisfied with Steven's version of the song. I think he left out the whole part about drinking and exchanged the message for some other message about love or eternal commitment or something. I don't remember. I think I was intoxicated from attending my own show.

At any rate, I corrected SCC's mistake and got it right. I can't tell you how many people have had this song at their weddings. I can't tell you because there have been none. C'est la vie, I suppose.

I Don't Drink Beer

When I'm out driving in my car I like to be able to steer
So I don't drink beer
When I try to communicate, I want
    for my words to be clear
So I don't drink beer

I don't drink beer, 'cause it doesn't make me feel well
And I need every brain cell I've been given
And I don't drink beer, I don't mean to be overcautious
But the bitter taste makes me nauseous
So I don't drink beer

When I'm out walking round the town, I
    don't want to fall down on my rear
So I don't drink beer

When I'm trying to ride a wave, I don't
    want to crash into the pier
So I don't drink beer

I don't drink beer, I don't need to head for the mountains
Or wake up in the mall fountain on Sunday morning
And I don't drink beer, I don't need an adviser
To know that Bud don't make me wiser
I don't drink beer

And when I'm giving my wife a hug, I don't
    want to throw up in her ear
So I don't drink beer
I don't drink beer
I like being sober
I don't drink beer

I actually think the best way to avoid the negative is to actively pursue the positive. It is statistically proven that students who are more involved in their churches, in sports, or in other extracurricular activities are less likely to abuse drugs or alcohol. In other words, stay active doing what is right and you won't have nearly the time to do what is wrong. Read books. Play football. Get together with your friends and play some games.

Go play outside like we used to do. Hopefully you will be more creative in coming up with games than we were as children. We only had a few games that were cool to play. Like Spin Around. I loved Spin Around. You just go out in your front yard and just spin around. When you get too dizzy, stop spinning around. Simple.

Ooh, and I wonder if anyone else remembers the classic game of Car's Coming? It's pretty self-explanatory. You stand in the street and wait until someone yells, "Car's coming!" On second thought, that wasn't the best game.

The best game was good old Hide-and-Seek. Oh man, I loved

Hide-and-Seek. Do you know why Hide-and-Seek was so good? Because all over the world, everyone plays this game exactly the same. Especially when you're "it." You always count while being out of breath from all the previous running. "Forty-eight . . ." huff huff . . . "Forty-nine . . ." huff huff . . . "Ready or not, I'm hyperventilating." I also loved Hide-and-Seek because you always had one friend who was terrible at it. You open your eyes and he's standing in the middle of the street.

"Dude, I see you. And for the last time, Mom said we can't play Car's Coming anymore."

And if you are not a huge fan of outside games, there are always inside games too. My only request is that the younger generation comes up with some better board games. We had horrible board games growing up because they always lie to you.

The game box will tell you the name of the board game and then give the accompanying description—and it's always a lie. Take Clue, for instance. "Clue: an exciting mystery game for the whole family." Tell the truth, man. It should be, "Clue: your younger siblings don't have one," or "Clue: TV will be time better spent."

They should have called another famous game by this name: "Battleship: learn how to hate your brother." Yep, that's closer to the truth.

Or "Trivial Pursuit: find out how dumb your dad is."

"Pictionary: the game that leads to divorce."

Or take Operation. Wow, that was the worst. I've often wondered which one of Satan's angels came up with that game. It provides a great message for any eight-year-old out there. "Operation: make a mistake and you'll get electrocuted."

"Hey Timmy, go for the bread basket."

"Mhhhmgh . . . Um, I think I lost. Let me check the rules. It says that if you're tasting metal, you lose. Okay, well I'm definitely tasting metal, so I guess I lose? Also, could you guys call an ambulance?"

Tweet Thought @timhawkinscomic

No, *Message* Bible, the phrase "Go big or stay home" was not in the Sermon on the Mount.

Tweet Thought @timhawkinscomic

The great thing about Ezekiel bread is you can eat it or use it to sand down a tabletop.

34

WHAM-O

I never want to be the voice of fear, but if I am being honest with myself, danger is lurking around every corner. It goes by many names and we all know them very well, even if we try to avoid speaking about them. Sickness. Injury. LEGOs. You know, all the usual suspects.

There are some dangerous toys out there. People need to be careful. I think the most dangerous toy has to be the glow-in-the-dark Frisbee, made by Wham-O. I call that foreshadowing. You see, I know the Frisbee glows in the dark. The problem is that the trees in my backyard do not.

Wham-O. That's the sound of my kid hitting a telephone pole. Hey Wham-O, why don't you make some glow-in-the-dark shrubs or potholes? Then I'll buy your fancy Frisbee. What's next? A glow-in-the-dark lawn dart? "Your turn, Jimmy. Jimmy? Ah dang it! Mom, I impaled Jimmy again. I know, I know. I'm going to go sit in time-out while we wait for the paramedics."

I always loved the thinking behind the Nerf ball. Little, lovable, harmless little Nerf ball. Wouldn't hurt anybody. That is until you attempt a diving catch across the living room into the glass coffee table.

If you've got little kids in the house, you must watch for the land mines—their little toys—buried deep in the carpet fibers of your house. It's like a midnight war zone at my house. I have no problem admitting to women that childbirth is the number one most painful thing a human can endure. You win. But I think the world needs to know about a close second: stepping on a single LEGO barefoot in the middle of the night while out on an innocent mission to get a drink of water.

Holy stinking moly. Those things could flatten the tires on a tractor trailer. Imagine a tiny piece of indestructible plastic gouging the soft tissue of your plantar fascia with no warning—it is a tale of a sole and a soul being destroyed simultaneously. There is no epidural for that little land mine. What was that, a box jellyfish? Did I unknowingly trod upon the head of a Gaboon viper? I think we should fight the terrorists with LEGOs—in fact, that is the basis for my future political campaign: Life, Legacy, and LEGOs—Terrorists Beware.

Of course I know that my children are not purposefully leaving things out on the floor simply to watch me injure myself and then laugh at my pain. That may be what my wife does, but not my children. They are not that smart—yet.

I love my children dearly. In fact, not too long ago, I made them breakfast. It was a full, balanced meal. It took me like an hour and a half to prepare this huge breakfast. I woke up early and got to work because I really wanted to surprise them. The best-laid plans and whatnot.

When it was all ready, I woke all the kids up and brought them to the table where their huge morning feast was waiting to be devoured. I envisioned impromptu applause and "For He's a Jolly Good Fellow" being sung spontaneously throughout the morning. Finally being friended on Facebook by my own children. Victory.

I continued to finish getting things from the stove when instead of these joyous songs, I heard, "Aaaahhhh!"

I ran to the table in a panic. "What's wrong?"

"There's pulp in the orange juice!" The kid was doubled over as if someone had pumped him full of lead. "Puuuulpppp! You got the orange juice with full pulp in it. Daddy, get it off my tongue—I'm choking!"

Get it out? Come and let us reason together. I've seen you eat an orange before. Pretty sure that's as "full pulp" as it gets. Now if there's ever pulp in the milk I give you, then you can freak out because I will agree that's not good. That's cottage cheese. But orange pulp?

It turns out that pulp is like Kryptonite to my kids. Not a bad thing to find out because now whenever I want to be alone, I just go into my office or bedroom—or what the hey, my bathroom—and smear pulp on the outside door knob before I close myself inside for some sweet solitude. Who knew a few fruity little shards could make a man so happy?

I wish making my kids this happy was as easy as a bathroom barricade. It is not. I have tried. Our four-year-old freaked out for the first few hours. When I finally opened the door because he had escalated past the point of reasonable preschool screaming, I realized we had accidentally left the lights turned off. A few popsicles and a couple spoonfuls of Benadryl later, all was well—and my son eventually felt better too.

But I do really want to make my kids happy. They are my treasures. My gifts from God—and there is no punch line following that fact. Well, not yet anyway. But I love them with all my heart.

So awhile back we loaded up and took the kids to one of the Six Flags theme parks. We spent the entire day riding coasters, playing carnival games, and eating. Funnel cakes. Bratwursts. Cheeseburgers. Deep-fried cheeseburgers. Dippin' Dots. Deep-fried Dippin' Dots—also known as warm sugar cream. Makes it harder to eat out of a cone, but once the sugar coma has set in, the kids hardly notice anyway.

We paid for stuffed bears. Stuffed dinosaurs. Stuffed rabbits. Stuffed children—see aforementioned description about the food purchases. Once the powdered sugar had settled, I had spent over half a grand—and it was truly worth every shekel—not to be confused with shackles.

Speaking of shackles, at one point I could have used a pair when that creepy-looking dancing Six Flags guy from the commercials approached us. You know the one. Black tuxedo. Red cummerbund. An obviously fake bald head. Obnoxiously thick, black-rimmed glasses.

I'm sure they created him to be a lovable caricature that kids will recognize and gravitate to.

Mission not accomplished.

Let me tell you, as our amazing day was coming to an end and Professor Promgeek walked up to us to dole out creepy hugs to our family, my kids were not ready to play that game. In fact, they should probably consider adding a seventh flag to the other six—a warning flag like the ones they put up at public beaches when there are dangerous conditions. Why? Because that guy was in danger. My youngest yelled, "Stranger danger!" and kicked that black-tied actor right in his Dippin' Dots.

As the sun was setting on a glorious day and the security detail was walking us out to the parking lot, my heart was full of joy. We were a family. Together. Broke. Delightfully sun-kissed with the beauty of the shared experience. My precious munchkins collapsed into their seats in the back of the car while my wife and I took our places in the front. We glanced at each other and exchanged that parental smile of contentment that requires no words.

As I gently took hold of the steering wheel and drove away reminiscing about the wonderful experience we had just shared, I heard something from the backseat that began to tighten my grip. It was the unexpected sound of whining. I attempted to keep things calm. I was sure they were just overtired and I did not want to overreact.

"Sweetie, what's wrong?"

"Billy's daddy took them to Disney World—and for a week. And we just got to go to Six Flags. For a day. We hate you!"

"Sweetheart, look up here at Daddy." Then I just let go of the steering wheel and theatrically broke out into song, "Jesus, take the wheel!" I know parents out there feel me. Hey, we've got insurance—let's just see what happens. Okay, so I didn't let go of the wheel for long, but I just didn't want to hear any more nonsense. How ungrateful could they possibly be? Disney World?

I think we parents should pool our collective resources and create a new theme park for kids. Instead of Disney World, we'll call it Third World. We'll drop them there for a few weeks and see if they don't come back with a little more perspective. I could just hear their theme song playing through the speakers built into plastered rocks all over the park, "It's the Third World after all . . ." It would be just like *Hunger Games*, except with less fun and more violence.

"Daddy, I want a Happy Meal!"

"We're at Third World. You'll be happy to get a meal, son."

"Daddy, is that Snow White and the seven dwarfs?"

"No, that's a missionary and seven pigmies. Move along."

"Look, Daddy. It's Mickey Mouse!"

"No, that's a giant rat. Run for your life!"

Tweet Thought @timhawkinscomic
There had to be toys in biblical times. GI Joseph. Stretch Armstrong of Arimathea. Easy Bake Fiery Furnace.

Tweet Thought @timhawkinscomic
Mr. Literal then proceeded punching himself in the face in an effort to fight back the tears.

35

I CAN'T BELIEVE IT'S NOT BUTTER

My life revolves around creativity, even when I wish it wouldn't. Ever since I was a kid, I've had this tendency to see the world differently than most people around me. I'm not gifted or anything. I just have a different viewpoint. When someone else sees blue, I see green. When others see half-empty glasses, I see salvageable free drinks—when you're not afraid of a little hepatitis, there's a whole world of possibilities. One man's trash is another man's takeout.

It is no surprise, then, that I naturally gravitate toward creative things in our culture. I'm fascinated by the fact that these companies and advertising agencies get paid to sit around and create stuff. What a dream. I'm here waiting tables and some dude in a suit is rolling around in piles of money right now just for fun—and all because he created the Nike swoosh.

First of all, no one actually knows what the Nike swoosh is. That's what's so brilliant about it. He made up something and then convinced everybody that it was something to the point that now everybody compares their own something to something that was nothing not too long ago. Isn't that something?

"What is that thing on the side of your shoe? A feather? A wing? A kickstand?"

"Dude. It's a swoosh."

"A swoosh? Isn't that what the toilet water does right before it goes down the hole?"

Nope. Swoosh is now a real word we all recognize because some guy somewhere had nothing but one simple idea—and the backing of a multimillion-dollar international corporation complete with marketing firms on retainer, tens of thousands of retailers and outlets, a string of international sweat shops, and celebrity athlete endorsers being paid millions to stand in front of the camera and say, "Just Swoosh It!" Later on, somebody accidentally changed the slogan after a dozen failed attempts to spell the word *swoosh* on the teleprompter. Finally a disgruntled director screamed at the errant speller, "Dude, just do it!" The rest, as they say, is history.

But back to my point, besides the few additional resources listed above, Dr. McSwoosh now has a giant ocean-view mansion complete with a heated doggy pool (which is the ultimate mark of sophistication) simply because he had a simple idea. Hey, I have simple ideas too. Where's my doggy pool?

And the real kicker is that I see products and advertisements all the time that are far from "swoosh worthy," yet still land people that pooch pool. The worst has to be "I Can't Believe It's Not Butter!" Seriously? First of all, I can't believe you would use that many words to name your product. Could you imagine if car companies attempted this strategy?

"Introducing the latest innovation in luxury. The new 2015 'Driving This Car Will Make Your Neighbors Jealous.' Named Best New Sedan by *Car and Driver* magazine and winner of the J.D. Power & Associates award for longest name in luxury class. Hurry in to your local 'We Put Our Young Children in Our Commercials to Trick You into Spending More Money' dealer today!"

I Can't Believe It's Not Butter? Seriously? That is not a name at all—it's an anti-name. It's not telling us what it is; it's telling us what it's not. Now that's not such a bad idea. I should have tried that in my wedding vows. "My sweetest love, instead of telling you all the things I will be to you—lover, protector, provider, listener—I think it might be more beneficial to tell you all the things I will probably not be. I will not be: attentive to your voice during football games, a cleaner of toilets, a listener to your directions while driving, and I will not be willing to share my cheesecake when you declined the opportunity to order your own. Now lean in here for a kiss, sugar plum. Sugar plum? I can't believe I'm not married!"

I doubt that anyone actually eating this product actually shares the sentiment on the label. "Oh no, I can't believe that this is not butter. I cannot even fathom it." My bet is they believe it—it says it right there on the label. And is anyone else besides me even a bit concerned that we have no idea what we are actually eating? All we know is that it's not butter. Seems like a smoke screen to me. "Well, I can't believe it's not butter—it could be lard-flavored dry hand cream, but who cares!"

I guess it works, though. I can think of quite a few other products that could use a good advertising diversion. Instead of rice cakes, they might call them "I Can't Believe I'm Eating Packing Material!" Hmm, maybe back to the drawing board on that one. Not sure there is a redeemable diversion for rice cakes. Perhaps "I Can't Believe I've Given Up on Happiness."

Spam might consider this marketing strategy as well. They could call their product "I'm Fairly Certain That Ain't Meat." How about Ramen noodles? "I Can't Believe I'm This Broke!" The possibilities are endless.

But the point is that we must demand a high standard for creativity. When we don't, people could get the wrong idea about our product. For example, there is a women's clothing store in our town that I believe has missed the target altogether. The actual name of the store is Dress Barn. That's the best name you could come up with there? I wonder what the employees at the Dress Barn are like. "Can I help yeeeeaaaooo? It's only twenty buck-buck-buckas."

"Were you raised in a barn?" No, but I shop at one.

My next string of thoughts about the Dress Barn must be put delicately. I sincerely hate to point it out, but most of the women I know are not very fond of the idea of being compared to any creature who may reside in a barn. I shall not name the actual names of the animals who live in barns as I would never want there to be any misunderstanding that I am in any way actually using these animal names in a derogatory manner toward any individual of the female persuasion or otherwise. Disclaimer: my legal counsel has approved this statement. I will just say that some of the animals have been known to "moo," "neigh," or even "oink." You do the barnyard math.

Who in their right mind would name a store that sells women's clothes after a place where such beasts of burden—or bacon—might bunk down for the night? I can only pray that it was a misguided female and not an undiagnosed male—and his diagnosis would most definitely be insanity. Nevertheless, the Dress Barn lives on in infamy and women come by the herd to shop there. "You want to try that on, ma'am? Here's the key to the changing stall. There's a shovel and some hay to clean up in there when you're done. Get along, little dogie!"

New name for the Dress Barn? "I Can't Believe I Got Stabbed by My Wife!"

New name for this book? *I Can't Believe It's Not Better.*

Tweet Thought @timhawkinscomic
I don't really know the back of my hand. I don't think I could pick it out in a police lineup.

Tweet Thought @timhawkinscomic
Don't judge a man till you walk a mile in his shoes, unless he's wearing those moronic five-toe deals that only idiots wear.

UNICORN LASER HORN

I make a lot of jokes about marriage, but that's exactly what they are—jokes. I am merely poking a little fun at something I treasure more than anything on this planet. Marriage should be fun—and will often be funny too. That's why I encourage married couples everywhere to keep dating their spouses. Marriage is the greatest gift God has given us, so get out there and have some fun together.

Like the other day when my wife and I decided to spend the entire day in bed. We laughed. Talked. Played games. We even had a crazy pillow fight. Then the mattress store manager told us to leave. We made a memory that day. We even had a laugh with the mall cop who escorted us out to our car.

Much like a successful trampoline, a successful marriage needs a little healthy tension—and perhaps some protective netting. Marriage is indeed like a trampoline in that sometimes people accidentally miss their landings on backflips and fall flat on their faces. Yep, I call that Valentine's Day. The key is to get back on the horse and keep on jumping. Wait, I think I just mixed my metaphors a little too much. Mixing too many metaphors at once is a dangerous game of cat and mouse that can leave people sliding down a slippery slope with no net to catch them at the bottom of the barrel in which fish are easily shot. I think you catch my drift. I've got to get my face in the game.

Tension. I took my wife out the other night and there was just a lot of tension. At this point in my life, I can admit the truth: it was my fault. I understand that. I brought it upon myself and I will probably continue to bring it upon myself for the unforeseeable future. "Til death do us part, I'm an idiot at heart." It's a new country song I'm working on.

We were driving on our way to eat dinner and the same fight that always occurs broke out right on cue. She was dressed up so nice—a picturesque image of beauty and sophistication. The mother of my offspring. The apple of my eye. All I want in life is to make her happy, so I asked a simple question that should have clearly communicated that not only did I care about her opinions, but I was listening. Are these not good things?

"My beautiful, elegant muse. Where couldst I direct our carriage on this fine evening in terms of establishments of sustenance that wouldst most capably gratify thine appetite?" I swear that's how I said it. I mean, I did shorten it a bit, something like, "What do you want to eat?"

"I don't care. What do you want to eat?"

"I don't care. What do you want to eat?"

This ping-pong match of indecision went on for about another seven rounds. I think all married couples understand this conversation and where it leads—nowhere good. Finally she said, "Will you just make a decision?"

"Okay, we'll have Italian then."

"I hate Italian."

Now all I wanted was whiskey. Just a jumbo double whiskey—is that a thing? Because that was all I wanted. As I said, there was just this tension. After the hot debate raged on a little longer, we came to a mutual agreement of sorts and I pulled the car into the parking lot of a restaurant.

We sat down at our table and the waiter asked us what we wanted. I turned to my lovely bride and continued to sensitively ascertain her wants and needs. "Honey, do you know what you want?"

A flustered expression broke out on her face like poison ivy. She turned to me and said, "Do you know what I want?"

At this point, I was waiting for the hidden cameras and the jocular reality television host to reveal themselves. "Tim Hawkins, you just got Marriage Mashed! Ha ha, you should have seen your face! Your wife set up the whole thing!" The cameras never came. You connect the dots of logic.

My wife continued. "I want you to want to know what I want."

I turned to the waiter and said, "We're going to need a few more minutes." He nodded his head and shot me a look of sympathy that said, "Hey man, I see you're stuck here, but helping you is above my pay grade. I'm going to retreat to the kitchen for a half hour."

It got worse. The waiter finally came back to actually take our drink orders. So I said, "Yeah, I want a Cherry Coke. Honey, do you want a Cherry Coke?"

"You don't even know who I am, do you? I don't like cherries. I don't like Coke. And I for sure don't like Cherry Coke. Does your girlfriend like Cherry Coke?"

"No," I replied, "she likes Pepsi."

The tension is not confined to restaurants. Sometimes my wife gets mad at me for behaving badly—in her dreams. Come on, that's not fair at all. Last week she said, "I had a horrible dream last night. Do you want to hear about it?"

"Hmm, you know, cupcake, I'm not sure we want to . . ."

"I'm going to tell you anyway. A grizzly bear was chasing me through the woods. His teeth were so sharp and he was growling at me so violently. He was going to eat me—and you did nothing."

I generally do not carry a mirror with me to see my own face during conversations, but I can only imagine the expression of complete helplessness. She continued.

"You just sat there and did nothing."

I finally decided to enter this maddening conversation and see if I could outrun the bear myself. "Okay, well, what was I doing?"

"What were you doing? You were playing poker with a rabbit. That's what you were doing. And that's the thing. You would do something like that. You would play poker with a rabbit while I was being eaten by a bear. Do you want me to die? Is that your plan?"

"Honey, you know that this was just a dream, right? Like there were not actually any bears or rabbits or—"

"Luckily, a giant unicorn swooped down and saved me with his laser horn. That's how I got saved. Not by you!"

Tension. There's just tension. I'm thinking of the tension that makes a harp string sound so beautiful. Or nuclear war.

Tweet Thought @timhawkinscomic
If he gives her a book, he's thinking, *She'll like it*. If she gives him a book she's thinking, *This'll change him*.

Tweet Thought @timhawkinscomic
Old dudes don't lose their hearing so much as they've mastered the habit of ignoring everybody.

OKLAHOMA SHAKESPEARE

One of my main reasons for writing this journal is to keep a record of what inspires me. I hear so many questions out there traveling on the road, but the most frequent one is, "Tim, where do you come up with your comedy?"

Honestly, I don't know. Inspiration comes in so many forms. Movies. Music. Family. Food. Comedy is a commentary on what everyone sees, but with a perspective most everyone does not see. It is an art form, similar to a magic trick. Some might even call it a gift. Comedians look at the same things normal people look at, and then point out the ridiculous part hidden in plain sight. It's like I always say—comedy is a dish best served with a dash of absurdity and a pinch of stupidity. I don't like to brag, but I am the Iron Chef of stupid.

Okay, I have to confess: none of my previous statements were true—or even comprehensible, for that matter. The truth is, when I need inspiration for comedy, I just take a drive through Oklahoma. Those people provide me with more ammo than what a doomsday prepper could get at a free shopping spree at an Oklahoma gun show. And that is true on so many levels.

Recently I was driving through Durant, Oklahoma, when I passed by a sign that read "Oklahoma Shakespeare Festival." Do you see what I mean? It's like the joke fishes jump in the comedy boat by themselves. Yep, I know when I am really in the mood to watch some quality Shakespeare, I look no farther than Durant, Oklahoma. What a hotbed of Shakespearean acting.

"Romeo! Romeo! Where ya at? Show yourself, hoss. I'm freezin' up here in these tights. And move yer truck. Daddy has to go to work in the mornin'."

But I must also confess that certain other states in our incredible nation also provide fantastic fodder for some head-scratching. I was in Mobile, Alabama, not too long ago and was waiting at the airport for my plane to arrive so we could board. I was looking out the window at the runway and a local guy walked up and said, "Man, those planes sure do come in low, don't they?"

Yeah, it's called a landing, bubba. There's really no other way to do that. "We're coming in for a perpendicular descent. Get off the plane if you're still alive." I would like to extend a heartfelt thanks to the confused stranger from Alabama who reminded me why I do what I do. I salute you, sir.

But there are other states that should be mentioned as well. I would call it an honorable mention, but that just seems inaccurate. A dishonorable mention? That seems a little too harsh. A dishonorable discharge? That has always sounded kind of gross to me. There are certain words you never want to hear from your physician. "Listen sir, you've got a real problem here and it's so disgusting that our team has diagnosed you with 'dishonorable discharge.' Now take these pills and get out of here so we can disinfect this room, you filthy animal."

Again, I would not go this far in describing this next state, but it does deserve a mention: Texas. I actually love Texas, especially as a Dallas Cowboys fan. I often find myself traveling across the great state of Texas, but it is so vast that I get lost all the time. I don't know if you heard or not, but everything's bigger in Texas— including the number of guys driving around lost and too stubborn to ask for directions. "Look, Frank, we're back in the desert again.

We're stopping to ask for directions or I'll call my sister and find my own way home."

All by myself, I decided to pull over to see if someone might confirm that I was obviously going the right way. I ended up asking this old dude for directions. If he was an example of the average Texan, then it may be time to spike the state water supply with some ginseng or something. "Sir, how far is it to this restaurant?"

"Aw, it's about twenty miles as the crow flies."

Well, thanks, Sitting Bull. I appreciate your help. Wasn't planning on taking the crow today; it's in the shop. How about "as the man drives" . . . you got those coordinates? Just use regular English—I don't speak Texan.

Now I have no particular beef with the southern dialect, mainly because my mom is a southern woman. She loves to use certain southern analogies that have little to no meaning to most common English speakers. Even though I don't know exactly what she's talking about most of the time, she has a way of somehow getting her point across very clearly. I think it's a matter of selling out to your idiocy—it's something I proudly inherited from her.

"It's hotter than a frizzle-frazzle on a dingle-dangle out here."

Is it now?

"Whew yeah, but inside it's colder than a goobie-goobie on a whizzle stick."

Wow, Mom. That's pretty cold—I think.

But actually, I'm pretty impressed with her ability to complete an open-ended analogy with such perfect timing and confident precision —even if her words are nonsensical. Nothing is worse than getting halfway into a good analogy and then stalling out. It's humiliating.

Just the other day, I was telling a story to a friend and I got caught in one with no exit strategy. "Man, that line at the bank was longer than a . . . normal line usually is . . . at a bank . . . as the crow flies."

Shame.

Tweet Thought @timhawkinscomic

Walmart is like Target's redneck, lottery-winning sibling.

Tweet Thought @timhawkinscomic

A friend told me he's so broke he "don't have a pot to pee in or a window to throw it out." Sort of glad we"re not neighbors.

MASCULINE SONGBIRDS

There are plenty of skeptics out there—people who have doubts about most everything. This is not a new thing and neither is it something that each one of us cannot relate to. You may not realize it, but there is skepticism in each of us, especially if we are parents. Do you actually expect your four-year-old to make it from the table to the counter with that full glass of red Kool-Aid? Dude, it ain't gonna happen.

So yes, we all have things to be skeptical about. This is true even in matters of faith. Being a Christian, I am far from a "blind faith" kind of guy. Some skeptics think all people of faith must turn their eyes away from education, books, or anything that challenges our viewpoints. But real faith is not an absence of real doubt; it is the presence of a real relationship.

That's why even though you may be skeptical about your kids, you never stop believing in them because you know them and love them. If this is true, just imagine what real faith in God can be like—he never spills the Kool-Aid. And just considering how much I do spill the proverbial Kool-Aid, yet still experience his fatherly love on a daily basis, my faith has the foundation it needs to survive the doubts I also possess. I'm not "drinking the Kool Aid" or closing my eyes to anything—I'm just opening them to more than just skepticism.

The odd thing is that most skepticism about God generally doesn't arise over issues that occur with God himself. They are usually more about issues people have with God's people. That's why the church (not the location, but the group of people who follow Christ) is constantly at the center of the discussion regarding faith and skepticism.

As a man who spends most of his time traveling to different churches, I have seen my share of good and bad things—and I still love the church. I love seeing people making difficult choices to love each other through imperfection. I love a place where I know I can be myself. I also love the popcorn and free Wi-Fi.

But I love the worship experience too. I know there is theological debate about music in the early church—that is, the Christian disciples who originally gathered in Jerusalem to worship. This was the early church, not the early service at one's church. One was led by fishermen, and the other is the favorite service for fishermen trying to salvage their Sunday out on the lake.

But despite the debates, we know that worship music—of some sorts—was a part of their experience just like it is a part of our experience today. How cool. The same truths we are singing today—mind you, often accompanied by microphones and electric guitar solos—were being sung two thousand years ago. It is as if each generation continues to write a new verse, but we've all been belting out the same chorus for over two millennia. Talk about getting a song stuck in your head.

That being said, I do sometimes wish I could lend a little wisdom to modern worship pastors out there. I just want them to help me help them help us. My wisdom, like Sylvester Stallone, is short but powerful. If I could speak to worship leaders around America, I would offer them the following advice.

First of all, it's Sunday morning. It's very early. A lot of us haven't even had breakfast. Therefore, could you sing a song just one time in your life in a key we can all sing in—something that a normal human can latch on to? You're the music major. Figure it out. I'm not Barry White, but I'm also not a Bee Gee. Could you try picking something in the middle of these two extremes? And if you're nondenominational, here's a little revelation: I'm not slain in the Spirit; I just ran out of breath, you sadist.

And despite the fact that I play a lot of rock guitar for a living, do you think we can mix in a few more hymns every now and again? Why? Because at least with hymns you know when the song is over. Back in the olden days, you could plan your day around a hymn. First, second, and fourth verse, and then sit down. Everyone knows the third verse of a hymn is chockfull of heresy. Go figure. But, as I said, at least you knew what to expect.

I love the modern worship songs, but sometimes you just don't know when they're going to end. When there is only one verse, obviously it must be repeated, but there should be a limit—like a doctor writing a prescription or a box of donuts not having a secret compartment inside that leads to another dimension in which donuts are as plentiful as the air we breathe. Donuts for air? That would be ridiculous. Delicious, but ridiculous.

If I were the worship doctor writing the prescriptions for modern worship leaders, besides the advice to comb your hair and lose the skinny jeans and mascara, I would say to watch the congregation a bit to know when to exit a song. Songs are like parking garages. You've got to pay attention to the signs or else you might drive around in circles for hours looking for the light of day, which, by the way, is a great name for a worship song. Sing it with me. "I'm looking for the light of day, I'm following all your ways. I'm looking for a way to escape, I'm reaching out for more of your grace." Now four more times. Or twenty.

But when you see someone leveraging themselves on the chair in front of them for support, then you know it may be time to pull the rip cord. They've been standing too long. Maybe do a song about kneeling or sitting quietly before the Lord. Or resting in his presence? The options are endless. Regardless of how you find and take the exit, my worship doctor prognosis is simple: sing two verses and call me in the morning. Or at least hand out some PowerBars and Red Bull.

And I mean that. Except the calling me part. If you start calling me all the time, I will take out a restraining order against you. Trust me, I know how it works. Just ask our worship leader at church. Do you know how difficult it is to see the lyrics on the screen from two hundred yards away? And if you use binoculars, it just reinforces the whole stalker vibe you are trying to remedy in the first place. But nevertheless, I think my overall point is clear.

I suppose I have one more beef with modern worship leaders—an expression I wish involved bringing someone a steak. Every time someone has a beef with me, I get nothing but their irritating complaints. Perhaps a little New York strip cooked medium with a loaded potato would soften the blow a bit. Would it kill you to bring a little A-1 to the roast every now and again? I know thoughts like these are rare nowadays, but I'm just so sick of getting grilled every time someone has a beef with me.

But unfortunately, my beef has less to do with actual beef and more to do with actual words people would actually say. Thus, it is a departure from the style of this book altogether. Worship leader, do you ever wonder why men seem to sing a whole lot less in church than the women? We've already covered the issue of singing the songs in the keys where only a castrato can sing. "Man, I thought being a high tenor was a big deal, but I think I just felt something pop in my loins."

But I think I know another reason why men sometimes struggle to keep singing along. These days, a lot of songs are written from a female's perspective of love. Men are not always attuned to the subtle nuances of femininity, so sometimes we just don't understand it. That's not necessarily our way of expressing love, so we just don't know how to sing certain parts of songs from a masculine viewpoint.

For example, songs these days have lines like: "I want to see your face, I want to touch your face." Guys are like, "What? I mean, I love him, but I don't want to touch his face. Come on, man, I brought a visitor here from our job down at the coal mine. Don't make me sing that."

Look, there's nothing wrong with it. I'm just saying that perhaps you should add to your repertoire a few more songs men could really sink their teeth into. You work on the melodies and chords, but I have a few lyrics to work with. How about,

> Watch the game with me, Lord,
> Just sit here in silence,
> No talking or questions,
> And fall asleep halfway through.

Yeah, now that stirs up my soul.

Or try taking the music from the song "Open the Eyes of My Heart" and make it this instead:

> Get me a Coke from the fridge, Lord.
> Get me a Coke from the fridge.
> Bring me some nachos . . .
> With jalapeños!

Men would be sprinting to church with songs like that. Singing like songbirds—very masculine songbirds.

Tweet Thought @timhawkinscomic
"I'm a picker, I'm a grinner, I'm a lover, and I'm a sinner" isn't the best answer to "What can you bring to this company?"

Tweet Thought @timhawkinscomic
Every time I see an "Employees must wash hands" sign in a public restroom I'm like "Thanks, but I can wash my own hands."

39

WHAT'S IN A NAME?

The question has often been asked, "What's in a name?" The answer is complex, to say the least. I can think of many names that mean many things, and I can think of many names that mean much of nothing. I can think of lots of things, which I guess is why you are reading my private journal, yet we are both acting like we don't know that I know that is what's happening. Please don't tell me, though. Ignorance is bliss.

Names. Names can mean so much. Take the Do It Yourself Network. Sure, they shortened it down to DIY, but an abbreviation cannot change the meaning of a name. I don't know about you, but in my house the words "do it yourself" are rarely uttered in moments of marital or family harmony. "Hey honey, I appreciate the fact that you cooked me this dinner, but my steak is a little tough. Do you think next time you could—"

Before the misguided husband can finish his misguided statement, his wife, now engulfed in the flames of matrimonial anger, rebuts his butt with, "Do it yourself!" And I rest my case.

But in the case of the name of this network, Do It Yourself has found a way to spin the name in a positive way. In other words, viewers pay their cable provider and spend their precious time learning to do the very thing most of us never want to hear. Imagine taking your seat at an expensive restaurant—I mean, a real classy place like O'Charley's or Waffle House.

Now imagine that you open up the menu—or in the case of Waffle House, turn over again and again the quadruple-laminated document.

I mean, what sort of abuse must a restaurant's menus endure in order for someone at the top of the Waffle House management to order a menu fortified with this level of protection? These things are indestructible. If there is ever a nuclear holocaust, the cockroaches that survive will still have something to read—and images of syrup-laden cholesterol to torture them in the postapocalyptic age. These things are like a cross between plastic, iron, and Kenny Rogers's Botox— again, indestructible. They are blasted from the local waffle mines and then forged in the grease mill fires of Appalachia. I think I hear an Alison Krauss song coming on—a haunting refrain having something to do with using the appropriate fire extinguishers for grease fires as opposed to other kinds of fires. At first glance, not very singsongy, but anything sounds better with a Dobro.

You could build a dependably sturdy bridge out of Waffle House menus. Am I exaggerating? You be the judge. Next time you sit down in a booth at Waffle House—and I suggest trying this before your shoes have time to get stuck to the floor—go ahead and attempt to rip one of the menus with your bare hands. The only thing faster than the normal steady stream of customers running for the nearest *baño* will be you running for the nearest first aid kit to find a roll of gauze to sop up the bleeding and as much antibiotic ointment (after all, it is Waffle House) as the law will allow.

Actually, I think I've watched a little too much *Breaking Bad* because I'm pretty sure there is no legal limit to the amount of over-the-counter antibiotic cream you can obtain. For this reason, you might want to self-police a bit on this purchase or you could end up in a very strange kind of debt that will be difficult to explain to your tax guy at the end of the year. "So Roger, you spent seven thousand dollars on antibiotic ointment? Did you go to Waffle House again? I thought we discussed this last year."

But as I regress from my digression, I again think about that moment you read your menu and turn to the waitress to order. "I'd like the steak and eggs, please. How do I want that steak cooked? Hmm, let's go with medium E. coli—you know, just a little pink, but not enough to kill me—just how I like it! Eggs over medium, please. And I'll take hash browns—doubled, covered, smothered, diced, chunked, and rumbled."

Rumbled is a new addition to their hash brown preparation choices—it's where they take the finished pile of hash browns and drop them into a bowl of batter, then deep-fry them, and then roll the whole thing up in seaweed-like sushi. It is named *rumbled* because of what it will later do to your colon.

But that's not the most shocking part. As your waitress rattles off your order to the gangly cook in Wafflish (it's a language akin to Klingon, but without the subtle sophistication), the cook (who himself recently received a personal score of 71 on a surprise health department inspection . . . and they normally only inspect restaurants, not individuals—they made an exception for him) looks you straight in the eye, points his spatula at your head, and shouts back with the slurred speech that comes from inhaling greasy fumes for twenty years, "Do it yourself!"

Thus, one man's million-dollar home improvement network is another man's Waffle House mental breakdown. I've seen it a hundred times—well, or just this once. The example is a little unique, to say the least. But the point is clear: a name can mean so many things to so many different people in so many different scenarios and so forth and so on.

Maybe that's why parents deliberate so long and hard over their kids' names. Look, I get it. These names will stick with these kids forever—for better or for worse. And as my great-uncle Snothead could attest to, it is often for the worst. And for the record, he always claimed it was pronounced "snow-*the*-add." Regardless of the phonetic interpretations, the whole issue could have been easily avoided by one or both of the parents taking just a little more time in said deliberation process.

Names are permanent. So is love. Therefore, much like a Reese's

Peanut Butter Cup, I decided to put these two beautiful ingredients together in the most creative way I could conceive of: by getting tattoos of my children's names. Nothing says "I love you" more than having a complete stranger in a back-alley tattoo parlor play a painful game of colored needlepoint using your bare flesh as his personal creative doily pallet. I think it was Shakespeare who said it best when he wrote the famous line, "If you ink us, do we not bleed?"

The truth is, I have three tattoos. Most people I meet want to know about them. The tattoo on my arm is of a guitar, which obviously symbolizes the important role of music in my life and career. I also have a tattoo of a dragon across my chest, which symbolizes my love of the church. Obviously I'm only kidding. It's on my back.

But my most important tattoo is the one I've already mentioned— the one with my kids' initials. As I told you, choosing children's names is so important and it requires a parent who possesses maturity, forethought, and wisdom.

That's why my wife named our kids.

She did a great job. She chose names that actually have meanings. It was no doubt a long and painful process, most only metaphorically. I got a tattoo, which hurt a lot more than choosing a silly name. Every time I tell her this, she reminds me about how painful childbirth was and I'm like, "That again?" So sick of having that whole "I carried little people in my body for nine months" thrown up in my face all the time. Oh yeah, and I've carried those little people ever since. My shoulders and your womb have competing war stories.

But at any rate, my tattoo has their initials. The *S* is for Spencer, which means "servant." We are hopeful that Spencer will feel the blessing of such a legacy and follow in the footsteps of those biblical and family members who exemplified true servanthood before him. He could start by doing a few dishes every now and again—or at least stacking a few chairs. I mean, seriously. If your name is "Servant," you need to own it.

The next letter on my tattoo is *O* for our Olivia. Her name means "peace." It's a perfect name for her, as just the other day I heard her mother say, "Olivia! I'm begging you for just one moment of peace, please—for the love of all things good and holy!" Yep, the perfect name for my girl. The *J* from my tattoo is for "Jackson," which means "son of John." Yeah, I'm still kind of working through that one. And finally, the *L* is for Levi, which means "leader." We actually believe Levi is going to be the president someday. Just to be safe, we have stowed away his birth certificate in a very secure location. We are prepared for all political contingencies.

I think it's hilarious when parents give their kids "spiritual" names. You know the type. The overeager churchgoing soccer mom who always wears khaki capris, a floral print tank top, and a headband that keeps her from ever having to wash her hair. This is a major difference between men and women. I wash my hair at least once a day, if not twice, depending on what activities I have done. I have known my wife to not wash her hair for three weeks. Hey, just pull that mess up in a headband and who—besides people with an active sense of smell—will ever know? I say live free.

But truthfully, I am a big fan of parents and I have immense respect for the challenges they face every day. Theirs is a pain I know well, as if we share poison ivy or lice. However, some parents are prone to think they can use names to keep their kids from being the animals that all children are. These parents want to think that their children are always little angels—yeah, more like Hell's Little Angels. They ride little Hot Wheels trikes with elaborate Ben-Hur chariot daggers jutting out from the center of the wheels.

"So, these are my little angels. This is Grace, Mercy, and Truth. They are just my everything. Oh, and little Justice is on the way," she says as she rubs her expectant belly. Listen, I know names are important, but give me a break. Why don't you name those kids after the way they really act?

"So this is Vengeance, Greed, and Sloth. And . . . Satan. Satan! Give back that man's wallet! *Satan!*" Then she rubs her belly and says,

"Oh, and little Deception is on the way."

I think we ought to name kids like we did thousands of years ago. If you think about it, when a young Greek mother named her son "Alexander the Great," it pretty much guaranteed that things were going to go well for him. I bet he always got picked first to be on the football team. He always got the girl.

Now his little brother, "Carl the Mediocre"? Not so much. That dude couldn't catch a football to save his life. Or a dead sheep or whatever they tossed around back then. Everyone knows that early Greek oblong balls were known as sheepskins, the predecessor of the now popular modern pigskin, which is not actually made of pigskins anymore. It's right there in your ancient history book.

But there's a reason I know so much about this name stuff. I eventually had to change my name because it carried with it such pain and stigma. If I heard it once, I heard it a hundred times. "Hey look, everybody. There's Timmy the Bed Wetter!"

Thanks a lot, Mom.

But do you know who gets the worst names of all? Grandparents. No one calls their grandparents by normal names anymore. Grandpa? Grandma? Nope, not a chance. It's all just Peepaw and Meemaw and Wa-Weewaw. That's my Noo-Noo and my Boo-Boo. And that's my See-Saw over there. My Goo-goo-goo-boo-doo-doo.

Once during a show, I asked the audience for some actual grandparent names that are used in their families. Somebody shouted out, "Koo-pop!"

Koo-pop? What is he, a teletubby? And when you ask people why they use these unintelligible names, they usually say, "Well, the baby couldn't say 'grandpa.' All he could say was 'Koo-pa-ca-poo-caca.' So now we just call him a string of indecipherable consonants and vowels ending with a clicking noise followed by a fart sound."

I understand the cuteness of our children and the need to let their voices be heard early on, but at some point in life, you've got to stop and look reality square in the eye. That precious creature you call your child, while beloved more than anything else in your world, is actually eating out of the flowerpot—and you're letting him name the patriarch of your family.

Come on, he's a homeschooler, man.

Tweet Thought @timhawkinscomic

Whoever named the fireplace was pretty lazy when you think about it.

Tweet Thought @timhawkinscomic

This morning I accidentally put my glasses on over my contacts. And when I looked in the mirror I saw my grandfather when he was a baby.

40

LAZINESS

Comedians are often stereotyped for being critical. Cynical. Mean. It's an unfair assumption and quite honestly, I don't like the stereotype. In fact, I hate it. And you know what? I think I kind of hate all the people who perpetuate it. Okay, so hate is a pretty strong word. Loathe. Yeah, that's better. I loathe them. Like to the point I'd put laxatives in their food and hang out in the stall next to them—waiting for hours if necessary. And I really don't like the friends of the people who spread these kinds of rumors about us. Or the cities they live in. Or what they stand for. Or their dogs. Or words in general. Or clowns. Man, I'd punch a clown right in his big fat red nose just to hear him honk. And I wouldn't feel bad about it. Laugh it up, Bozo. Who won the Grand Prize Game now?

But seriously, the only thing I hate more than clowns are these stereotypes about comedians.

Truth is, I do have opinions. However, I don't fancy myself as one of those guys who rants into a microphone about the issues in our world without actually being a part of the solution. Just the other day, I drove by this parking lot where a youth group was holding up hand-written signs that had the words "Free Car Washes," and just below it, "Donations."

I was blown away by their passion. So I let them wash my truck—they did a great job. Then they held out a bucket full of cash and I grabbed a donation out of it. I'm not real sure how they are going to pay for their missions trip with that kind of generosity, but I was just happy to do my part in such a worthy community cause. I couldn't really hear everything they were yelling as I drove away, but I could tell they were very moved by my actions as they were flinging their wet sponges in the air. Look, I'm no saint, but why can't more people out there just open their eyes to the needs around them?

So yes, I try to help when I can, which is why I feel more comfortable speaking up about an issue I think is bringing down our society. Honestly, besides clowns and candy corn, I consider it to be the scourge of our time: laziness. It is all around us and it is high time we wake up and see the truth before it is too late.

It is hard to admit, but I have witnessed firsthand how laziness can affect a family. Growing up, my brother was the second laziest individual in the world. Of course, the grand prize goes to whomever it was who named the fireplace.

"What's that?"

"It's a place where you put a fire."

"What do you call it?"

". . . a fireplace."

Sure this information about my brother might make Thanksgiving dinners more awkward, but honestly, with Uncle Roger's rare combination of narcolepsy and telekinesis, could it really get any weirder? Last year he fell asleep and dropped Grandma from ten feet.

So I'm unafraid to air out our family's dirty laundry—and also to talk some about the hidden embarrassing issues we face. And honestly, I would rather wash the clothes before hanging them up to dry, but that's another discussion for another time, I suppose.

When we were younger, my brother would never throw out a milk jug. He would empty it out and then put it back in the fridge. I would try so hard to reason with him. "Dude, put it in the trash can. There's nothing in it."

To which he would reply, "No, there's stuff in it. There's still milk in there."

So I would position it under the light to test his theory. "Hmmm, you mean that thin gloss right there at the bottom, hoss? Oh, you're right. There is milk in there. And that is very useful because I was going to have a single corn flake later. And this nanoliter of milk is really going to get it nice and soggy."

But laziness is not confined to one person in a family. I hate to admit it, but sometimes I feel it rising up in me as well. Nothing triggers it more than going to fill up my car with gas. I always use that little kickstand thingy on the nozzle to automatically pump the gas. But then every once in a while, it will be broken.

My reaction proves my point because the lack of that little piece of metal and plastic transforms me into a completely different person. An irrational person. An angry person. Okay, so maybe it's more of a continuation than a transformation, but standing at the pump actually holding that handle down the entire time feels like torture. "What are we, in the Middle Ages or something? Let's go. I'm going to get carpal tunnel here. I wanted to sit in the car while it was pumping and listen to my motivational tapes."

And my laziness leads to impatience at the gas pump as well. I usually prepay for my gas, handing the very helpful cashier ten bucks or so. Well, that's after waiting seventeen minutes for the people buying cigarettes or lottery tickets to get out of the way. What are they doing up there, undergoing a lie detector test or a federal background check? What could possibly take so long? Just order your nicotine and waste your money, for the love of Pete.

"Yeah, I'll take a Lucky Lotto, a Stupid Stewardship, and a Micro Money—no wait, make that a Macro Money." Yeah pal, like it really makes a difference. I'm not offended by your purchase; I'm offended by the massive waste of all of our time your purchase is causing. I just want to pay for my gas. I think they should make two lines at the gas station: a gas line and a vice line.

Once I have finally made it through the line and I begin pumping my gas, I feel better. The numbers on the machine just fly by, which makes me feel like I'm accomplishing something. All is well until, for some mysterious reason, the numbers reach the last gallon I have paid for.

What's that all about? $9.91 . . . $9.91 and a half . . . $9.91 and three-quarters . . . $9.91 and fifteen-sixteenths. Is the automated computer inside the machine afraid it might go over? You know what? Keep your eight cents because I've got things to do. Yes, my drive-offs at the pump are much different from most people who speed away from the pump. I actually leave the money and run. I don't know why I can't get my criminal career off the ground.

But if I was actually going to try to steal from gas stations, I think I would begin in Florida. From my observations after many years of traveling, this wonderful state seems like the easiest target.

I was in Florida the other day and I saw a sign on the gas pump that read "Do Not Siphon Gas with Your Mouth." Seriously, Floridians? Do you need that sign? I can just see some "ol' boy"—not to be confused with his dog, "Ol' Roy." "Well, I put my card in and I flicked that switchy thing . . ." He pauses for a moment to contemplate the reasons this magical gas contraption is not producing any gas. Then, suddenly an idea hits him over the head like a folding chair at a wrasslin' match. "Maybe I need to siphon this gas with my mouth? Yep, seems to me that the next logical step in this sequence would be me sucking on the end of this nozzle." I'm not sure that's as much laziness as oxygen deprivation at some level—the brain level, to be exact.

Even my home builder is struggling with the issue of laziness. I think they are unwilling to do some of the reasonable expectations that go along with building homes these days. My feelings are fresh on this issue, as we are currently building a house. And actually, it's going well. And when I say it's going very well, I mean *Aaaahhh!* These people are nickeling and diming us to death—an expression that I don't understand since I've hurled quite a few coins at my brother and I have never been able to even induce a coma, much less death. These aphorisms really need to have credible sources before they are launched out into the collective cultural lexicon.

At any rate, the sign for the construction company read "Homes starting in the 200s." But be not deceived, for a start does not a finish make—saith Yoda. I start things all the time that I don't finish. The laundry. The dishes. Sometimes I will start a sentence and never

So starting means nothing. Hey, I started a diet three days ago, but today I ate some ice cream cake. Sorry, I left out a word. I meant to say that I ate some dude's ice cream cake. Now I'm bloated and I'm wanted by the law. Well, for an old unpaid parking ticket, but you still get the idea. I don't think they'd put out an APB just because some kid's TCBY went AWOL down at the YMCA—if you catch my DRIFT. That last one meant nothing.

But anyway, the home we started building was supposed to be in the two hundred thousands. We've since moved up into the five hundred thousands. And counting. But it's not what you think. We are not throwing money around like it's going out of style. Which I wonder if that's why they keep redesigning certain denominations of our nation's currency—like the new twenty-dollar bills, for instance. Maybe money really is going out of style.

But my point is that we are not just spending tons of money on frivolous things. We have not added any granite steam rooms or Spanish hanging gardens; neither have we added Spanish steam rooms or granite hanging gardens. No indoor swimming pools complete with separate changing rooms where a team of tuxedoed butlers with British accents are waiting around the clock to hand you a towel, a robe, and an after-pool mint, as they ask you, "Is your bum quite dry, my lord?" Not that I want someone to care about that, I just think the word *bum* sounds hilarious in a British accent.

But there would be no helicopters, or helicopter landing pads for that matter. There is no way you can have a helicopter and stay in the two hundred thousands. Believe me, I asked.

I guess I am simply trying to communicate that the construction company did not tell us certain things when we signed up to start building a house in the two hundred thousands. We recently sat down to chat with a lady who worked for the builder. She sat at her computer and said, "Okay, today I just want to simply go over some of the options for upgrades for your house—if you want them. Now remember, these are by no means necessary and you don't have to do them. They are simply options. That's all."

We were so relieved to hear her tone because we were looking to save money and did not want someone trying to sell us a bunch of stuff we actually didn't need. No one wants to get taken when it comes to dropping that kind of moola. The builder lady continued as she pecked away at her keyboard. "Okay, let's see here, I'll just throw some options out here to get us going. Are you going to be wanting . . . doors?"

That's when I internally prayed and thanked God that I never followed through on getting that handgun carry permit. "Uh, yeah? I think doors would be nice, don't you, darling?" My wife did not reply. She was somewhere in her own catatonic state of mind, no doubt fantasizing about violence in much the same way I was. We share so much—that's why I love her: she wants to hurt people just as much as me.

The builder representative continued as if we weren't even there. "All right then, doors will push you guys into the three hundreds. And how about running water? Will that be something you'll want as well? I see a lot of the younger couples getting that these days."

Does the house come with a whiskey fountain? I think I may need one of those.

Tweet Thought @timhawkinscomic
I could totally live off the land, as long as there was a fully equipped chalet on said land.

Tweet Thought @timhawkinscomic
A nappy poo is better then a poopy nap.

THE JESUS FISH

I think if you're a Christian, then you're an ambassador for Christ everywhere you go. Even in the car. Contrary to popular theological belief, you don't get a pass in the car. Look, we all know someone who thinks they are exempt, but the truth is, no one is exempt. No one has a free pass. Maybe you even think that you do, but you really don't. No one does. Absolutely no one.

I do.

I have no problem admitting that I have road rage. I confided to my accountability partner about it, which in the Christian world just means a close friend whom you ask to verbally punch you in the stomach every now and again when you need it. I know—more violent and less creepy than the term denotes.

My accountability partner spoke this wisdom to me: "Well, just pray when you get mad." That sounded like a great idea. It was a perfect dose of holy wisdom. So I tried it. It didn't work out like I expected. Put it this way—if Jesus had a buzzer button he could push every time I do something absolutely stupid, I would have heard a huge *aaannnck!* right in my heart.

My vehicular holy time almost became vehicular homicide. I'm just a hypocrite. I was driving and the lady in front of me began braking as we were approaching a green light. You know, as if to anticipate it turning yellow so she could slam on her brakes and cause a rear-end collision—because some people do not actually want to make it through a green light. Not to mention that her unnecessary slowing

201

down meant I would probably not make the light. "It's green, Grandma. Gun it and let me get to church already!"

Fury began rising within me, but instead of letting a certain "finger" do the talking as I was tempted to do, I let prayer rise within me as well. But I must tell you, I don't think my heart was as in it to the degree that God probably prefers when people pray. "Oh Lord. God. Lord Jesus, help me now. Father, I just want to pray for this woman in front of me who seems to have a problem with *acceleration*. I really want to give her a holy *honk honk*. Could it possibly be in your will, Lord?"

He didn't answer. I don't blame him.

Apparently I'm not the only person of faith driving like a person of fury. I was recently cut off by a car on the highway and I almost wrecked into a ditch. As the guy sped off down the road to his Idiots Anonymous meeting or his latest court appearance or wherever he was going, I could see that there was a little silver fish on the back of his car. Now I'm not here to judge his Christian walk; it's his Christian drive I have a problem with. If you don't like driving like Jesus, take him off your car.

I don't know, put a little silver pitchfork on the back of your vehicle for a while. Make it more accurate and let people know what god or demigod you serve and that you're coming . . . that you're coming— and, as Wyatt Earp said in the epic movie *Tombstone*, hell's coming with you. I just think that for a road rager, a Christian fish is a bad witness. Speaking of witness, you may end up needing witnesses to testify in court because you got out of your car to scuffle with an old lady at a stoplight.

A fish on the back of cars should be a sign of unity among Christ-followers, but even then, I think everyone out there needs to be realistic about the fact that just because you see two cars with the same fish, those two cars still contain completely different people on the inside. Christians come in all shapes and sizes.

The Christian fish on the car is fairly unique because of culture's different iterations of this theme. Usually it's the other way around.

The Darwin fish predictably made its appearance not long after the Jesus fish. Fish with legs. Then the bumper wars began. The Jesus fish soon had the word *truth* written on the inside. Then the Darwin fish had *science* written on the inside. Then it reached a sort of critical mass and exploded into absurdity. The appearance of a Jesus fish devouring a Darwin fish. Wow. There's some good, solid biblical teaching for you. If somebody disagrees with you, *eat them*. That's right, what would Jesus do? Eat a Pharisee? Hmm. Only in *The Message* Bible, not in reality.

One of the reasons I love what I do is I get to meet people and go places I never thought I'd go. Not too long ago, I performed at my first Catholic church. I was a little nervous because I'm a Protestant and I had no idea what to expect. I didn't know if they would understand me or not, so to break the ice, I spoke my opening remarks in Gregorian chant—and in a perfect key of F. Seemed like a good Catholic key. "Hoooow's everyyyybodyyyy dooooo-iiiing? It's so nice to be here with yoooooouu toooooooniiiiiight."

I think they understood me and that they even liked the show. As one of them was standing up from his kneeling position, I heard him say, "This guy's good. I wasn't expecting him to be good." I get that a lot. Yep, much like my goal to do less and less work around the house, I exceeded expectations. Besides, everyone needs to laugh—especially at themselves. But it's like I always say: if you can't laugh at yourself, laugh at the Catholics.

Christians are such a diverse group. A lot of people criticize us for this, but the Bible actually celebrates the differences because we are a complete body with completely different parts. The differences are what should make it work best. Being a whole body that is only one body part is not only creepy, but also ineffective. Could you imagine a body that was nothing but an eye or an elbow? Talk about being all ears—a healthy body needs diversity.

So the week after my Catholic show, I was at a Pentecostal church, which is totally at the other end of the spectrum. Just like my Catholic friends, it was a blast and the people were very cool. But my Baptist mom felt the need to warn me about these guys before I did the show. She never said a word about my egg allergy before sending me off to work at a chicken farm, but she felt it necessary to warn me about Pentecostals. Thanks, Mom.

"Now Timmy, Pentecostals do things different from what we do."

"They do, do they? Do tell."

"Well, Pentecostal women don't cut their hair—and they don't wear pants."

"Really? They don't wear pants? That's probably going to be a bit distracting, don't you think? I certainly didn't read that in the contract. I guess I'll pray about this and get back to you."

But I love the way different people from different backgrounds of faith pray in different ways. Across the denominational board, I have come across people who love to pray what I call "thesaurus prayers." Of course I would never make fun of someone praying—to their face. But these people really rack up the word count without changing the content of the prayer at all. Their prayers continue, but any original thought in them does not. The upside is that all the other prayer participants get a chance to work on that less popular fruit of the Spirit known as long-suffering.

I was backstage recently with a pastor who was a thesaurus pray-er. I almost missed my cue to go on stage. "Lord, guide us. Lead us. Direct us. Navigate for us."

Come on, dude. But he continued, "Lord, guard us. Protect us. Be a shelter for us."

Dude, you've said like three things in three thousand words—and they all mean the same thing. Finish. Wrap it up. Conclude. I got things to do, bro.

That's the thing about church people and churches in general—they each have their own distinct personalities. With my job, I have to be sensitive to this because you never know who might be in the room.

Liturgical. Moderate. Charismatic. Asthmatic—those people come to church really needing a breath of fresh air.

But personally, I go to a church that is very expressive. It's a non-denominational. We can't decide on a denomination, because we like a little bit of everything. However, I'm not ashamed to say that it's a hand-raising church. Actually, I was amazed to find out that Catholics raise their hands in church too. To yell, "Bingo!"

At any rate, you may not go to a hand-raising church, which is fine, but if you were to visit, you may want to participate in what we're doing. You should feel free to do so, but I suggest not just jumping right in full force. I know it looks easy, but it's more dangerous than you think. Trust me, I've seen too many people carted out of the sanctuary on stretchers.

Start slow. We have a lot of different hand raises that we use. In fact, we actually have names for each of them. I have created a chart (on the following page) to walk you through what they are (please excuse the crudity of this model). And be sure to stretch adequately before attempting these. Happy holy hand-raising. Which oddly sounds like something Batman would say to Robin. You get the point.

Tweet Thought @timhawkinscomic
The frog into a prince story would have been way too long if Darwin wrote it.

Tweet Thought @timhawkinscomic
Saw a sign for "Christian Eye Care." Wondering if they specialize in plank removal.

THE TIM HAWKINS HANDBOOK
OFFICIAL WORSHIP SIGNALS
NON-DENOMINATIONAL

ROOKIE

ELBOW FLAP

CARRY THE TV

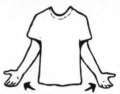
GO BIGSCREEN

MEDIAL

MY FISH WAS THIS BIG

HOLD MY BABY

MUFASA

PRO

DUELING LIGHTBULBS

GOALPOSTS + HEARTBURN

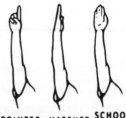
POINTER   HATCHET   SCHOOL ROOM

EXPERT

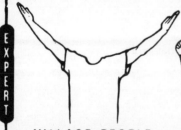
VILLAGE PEOPLE

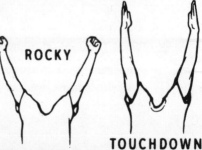
ROCKY

TOUCHDOWN

WARNING: VIOLENT HORIZONTAL MOVEMENT AND THE WAVING OF OVER-SIZED FLAGS ARE STRICTLY PROHIBITED AND WILL RESULT IN IMMEDIATE EJECTION.

FINAL THOUGHTS

I know the end of this book is now upon us. You're expecting me, as a Christian, to bring it all around and get spiritual. Turn the corner. Pass the offering bucket. Give me your e-mail address. Truth be told, I've given you so much and you just continue to sit there and take, take, take.

Don't be embarrassed. I feel the same way in my life. I've been surrounded by so many people who do nothing but give, give, give. Two loving parents who, to my knowledge, have never had a coarse word to say about their son. And I forgive you, Dad, for thinking it funny to fake heart attacks in front of me at five years old. A brother who, as my manager, gives the full weight of his enormous talents to share with me in this dream of whatever it is you call it that we're doing. Four kids who give me constant entertainment knowingly and unknowingly, and more joy than they will ever know. A wife who gives me something to long for, and fight for, and live for. And God, who will never be out-given.

Thanks, God, by the way. For showing me this whole gospel thing isn't so much about walking with you but resting in you. And thank you for your church, even the ones in it who make crappy judgmental bumper stickers and breath mints with scriptures on them. And sorry for the times I didn't capitalize the Y when I write something about You. I know You probably don't mind, but still.

Final Thoughts

And when all is said and done, three truths emerge in my life:

1. Be kind.
2. Embrace failure.
3. Never, ever eat two Fiber One bars at one sitting.

That last one is crucial. Stick that in your spiritual pipe and smoke it.

ABOUT THE AUTHOR

Since giving up his job as a grocery truck driver in 2002, Tim Hawkins has been meticulously crafting a no-bones, no-bull comedy show that entertains the entire family. With three hundred million online video views, over one hundred sold-out concerts every year, and a motley half million Facebook fans, Tim's Jackwagon Crew has grown into a gut-busting revolution of multigenerational proportions.

Tim's approach to comedy can best be described as one part gifted and two parts twisted. And the three parts set him apart. His stand-up is surgical and honed to perfection, bringing to light the brokenness of human nature while marveling in its hilarity. In his own gracious words, "If you can't laugh at yourself, laugh at other people." His musical dexterity and knack for parody stand on their own, as he deftly rattles off everything from Dylan to Aldean to brilliantly weird original songs.

The perils of marriage, parenting, and homeschooling may not exemplify the rock star life, but they make for rock star comedy. Still, Tim is no rock star: "It's not like I have choice. Comedy is my only life skill."

That's the Worst, Tim's latest DVD, is his seventh independently produced concert video. *Diary of a Jackwagon* is his first book.

Tim and his wife, Heather, live in Missouri with their four crud muffins.

ABOUT THE WRITER

John Driver (@john_driver) is an educator-turned-pastor who has authored or coauthored more than a dozen books. He founded Ignition 7, a unique initiative of videos and resources to creatively equip individuals for survival and longevity in faith. He lives near Nashville with his wife, Laura, and their daughter, Sadie. More at johndriver.com.